EXPLORING
SCIENCE *Six*

by **Walter A. Thurber**

Edited by **Paul E. Smith**

ALLYN AND BACON, INC.

Boston   New York   Chicago
Atlanta   Dallas   San Francisco

1959

EXPLORING SCIENCE SERIES

One · Two · Three · Four · Five · Six

READING
CONSULTANT

Linda C. Smith

Contents

Illustrated by
Philip B. Parsons
Charles E. B. Bernard

Plants That Are Not Green

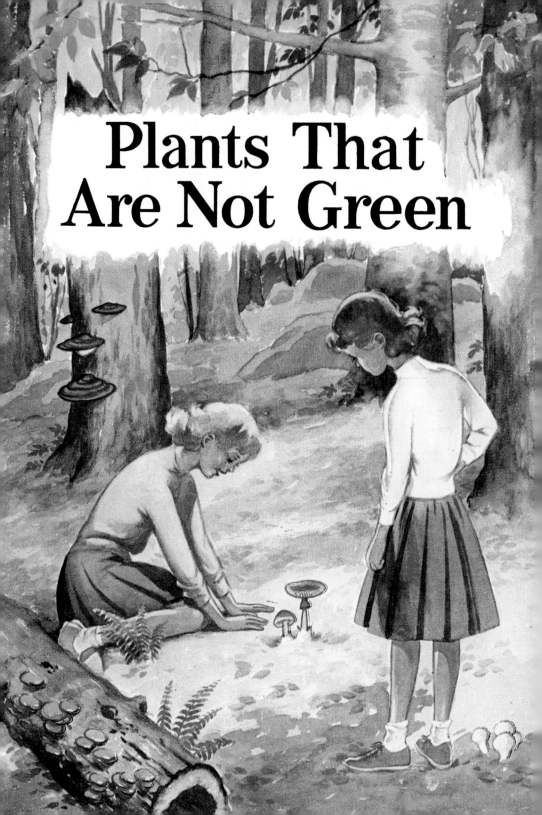

Finding Mushrooms

There are many plants that are not green.
Betty and Mary found some of them on a walk
in the woods one day.

"Look at the mushrooms," Betty said, pointing to some yellow plants growing among the
dead leaves on the ground.

"There are more of them on that log," said
Mary.

"They look a little like shelves."

Betty pointed to other mushrooms growing
on a tree trunk.

"Mushrooms can grow on live trees, too,"
she said.

5

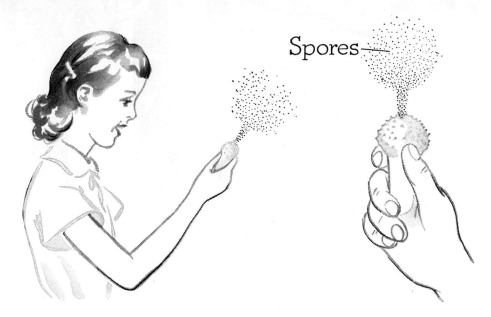

Spores——

Spores of Mushrooms

Betty found a mushroom that was shaped somewhat like a ball.

Mary said, "I know what that is. Pinch it."

Betty pinched the mushroom. The top popped open and out shot a cloud of brown dust.

"That's a puffball," said Mary.

The brown dust that came from the puffball was made of **spores.** Spores are somewhat like the seeds of other plants. Each spore can grow into another puffball plant.

6

Puffballs

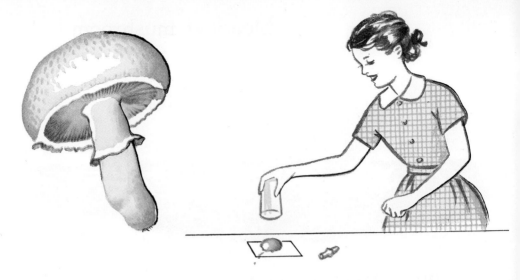

Other mushrooms have spores, too. Find a newly opened mushroom like the one shown above. Cut off its stem and lay the top part on a sheet of white paper. Cover it with a drinking glass and leave it overnight.

Then take away the glass and lift the top of the mushroom very carefully. You should see on the paper a print that looks like the underside of the mushroom. The print is made of spores that fell from the mushroom.

All mushroom plants grow from spores. The spores blow from the mushrooms. If a spore is blown to a place where it can grow, it grows into a new plant.

7

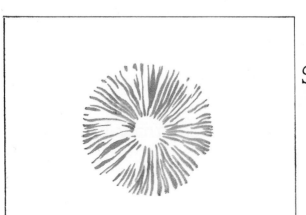

Spore print

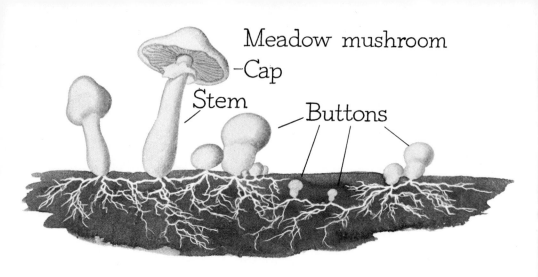

Meadow mushroom
-Cap
Stem
Buttons

What Mushrooms Are

A mushroom is only a part of the mushroom plant. It is somewhat like the fruit of other plants.

Most of a mushroom plant is hidden. It does not need light as green plants do. You can find the plant by digging around a mushroom. The plant looks like a mass of white, shining threads.

At times, little "buttons" begin to grow on the threads. These buttons grow rapidly. Sometimes they grow up out of the ground in a single night.

Then the buttons open and the caps spread out. There are millions of spores in each cap. The spores fall out and blow away. Each spore can become a new plant if it lands in a place where it can grow.

8

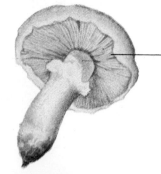

Spores grow here

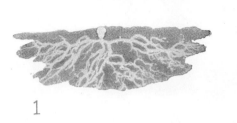

1

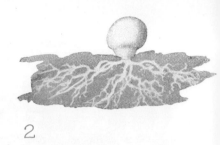

2

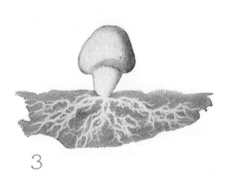

3

4

5

Spores———

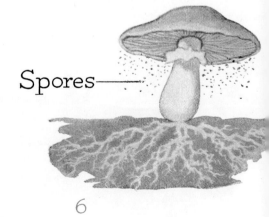

6

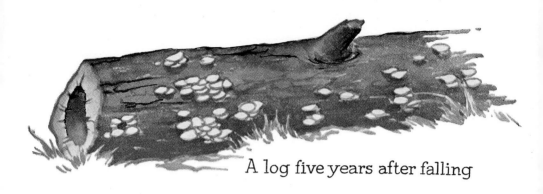

A log five years after falling

The Food of Mushroom Plants

Mushroom plants cannot make their own food. Green plants can use water, air, minerals from the soil, and energy from sunlight to make food, but mushroom plants must get their food from other things.

Most mushroom plants get their food from dead plants. Many of them live in dead wood. Others live in soil that has dead leaves, stems, and roots in it.

These mushroom plants are important. They break up dead plants and change them into rich soil. Green plants need this kind of soil.

Visit a woodland. Look for tree trunks and piles of leaves that are changing into soil. Collect some of the soil and study it with a hand lens.

The same log ten years later

Mushroom plants can also be harmful. Some kinds grow in living trees. Other kinds live in logs and lumber if the wood is damp.

We must often put wood in damp places. Fence posts and telephone poles are set in holes in the soil. Railroad ties lie on the ground. Floor beams of houses and barns are near the soil. When mushroom plants grow in this wood, they weaken it.

Wood used in damp places is sometimes soaked in chemicals that kill mushroom plants. Look at some telephone poles. Notice the black chemical that is used to keep them from decaying.

11

Fly Amanita

Poisonous Mushrooms

Some kinds of mushrooms are deadly poison if a person eats them. There are other kinds that make a person very sick.

The mushrooms you buy in stores are safe to eat, but it is not wise to eat wild mushrooms unless you know which ones can be eaten without harm. There are no rules that will help you tell a poisonous mushroom from a safe mushroom. You should never eat mushrooms that you do not know about.

Poisonous mushrooms will not harm you if you touch them. They are dangerous only if you eat them.

12

Destroying Angel

Deadly Amanita

Fairy Ring Mushrooms

These interesting mushrooms grow in circles on lawns and pastures. People have wondered about them for hundreds of years and they have made up stories about them. Some people once believed that the rings were places where fairies danced at night. They thought it was lucky to have them on their land.

Today we believe that a fairy circle started from a single spore. Each year the plant grows outward a little farther. The mushrooms grow only on the outer part of the plant.

You may not find rings that go all the way around. More often you will find parts of rings.

13

Fairy Ring mushrooms

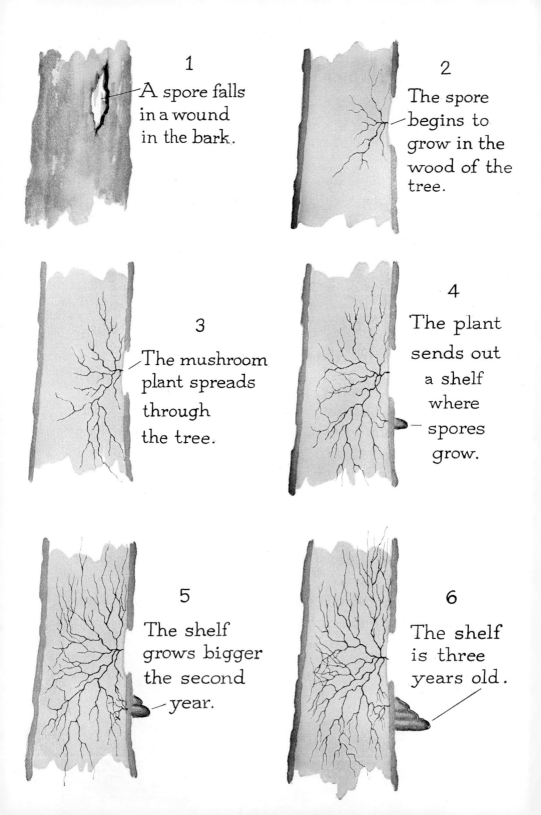

1
A spore falls in a wound in the bark.

2
The spore begins to grow in the wood of the tree.

3
The mushroom plant spreads through the tree.

4
The plant sends out a shelf where spores grow.

5
The shelf grows bigger the second year.

6
The shelf is three years old.

Shelf Mushrooms

There are several kinds of shelf mushrooms. Some kinds live in dead trees. Some kinds are found in living trees.

Some of these plants make new shelves each year. Other kinds add new layers to the bottoms and the edges of the old shelves. You can tell the age of one of these shelves by counting the rings or by breaking it open and counting the layers.

It does not help a tree to break off a shelf. The main part of the mushroom plant is inside the wood. The shelf is somewhat like the fruit of a plant. The plant is not harmed when the shelf is broken off.

15

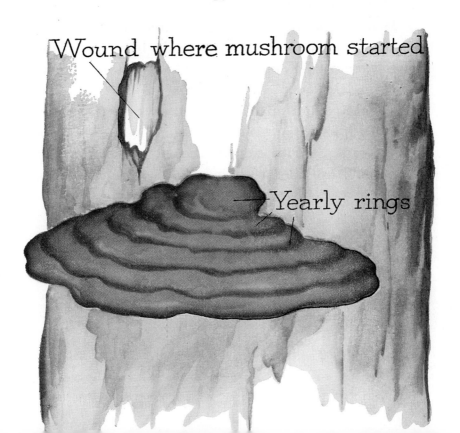

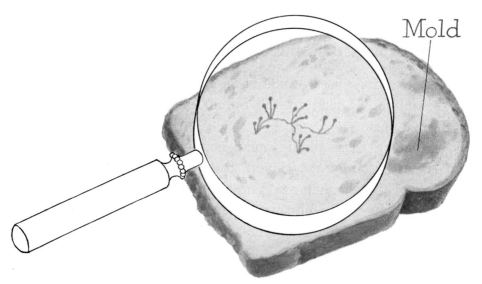

Mold

Mold

Have you ever seen mold growing on food? On what kinds of food have you seen it growing?

Mold is another plant that cannot make its own food. It must use the food made by other plants. Bread mold uses starch in bread. What plant made the starch?

A mold plant is made up of tiny threads that cover the food it uses. At times little branches grow up from the threads. Knobs grow on the ends of the branches. The knobs are filled with spores.

16

Spores

Mold gives off chemicals that flavor the food it grows on. Sometimes we do not like these flavors. We do not like the flavor bread mold gives bread. We do not like the flavors that molds give jam and jelly.

We like some of the flavors that molds give foods. We like the flavor that some kinds of molds give cheese. Fresh cheese is like cottage cheese. This fresh cheese is mixed with certain kinds of mold, and then it is put away to "cure." While it cures, the mold grows and gives the cheese a special flavor. Each kind of cheese mold gives a different flavor.

17

You can raise bread mold on a slice of bread. Put half a slice of bread on a plate and leave it uncovered for ten minutes. Mold spores in the air will fall on the bread during that time. Then moisten the bread and cover it to keep the moisture from evaporating. Look at the bread a few days later.

Try some experiments to find out what makes bread mold grow best. Use a slice of dry bread in your first experiment. Leave the slice uncovered for ten minutes. Then break the bread in two parts and moisten one piece. Cover both pieces with drinking glasses and leave them for a few days. Does the mold grow better on the dry bread or on the moist bread?

18

Dry bread   Moist bread

Find out if mold needs light to grow. Uncover a slice of bread for ten minutes. Put half the bread under a bowl and the other half under a drinking glass. In which place does the mold grow better?

Find out whether mold grows better in a warm place or a cold place. Perhaps you can keep the bread in a very hot place, also.

Mold plants are killed if they are heated to the boiling point. One way to keep fruit from spoiling is to bring it to a boil and put it in tight cans. Then mold spores cannot get to the fruit. What fruits are preserved this way?

Mold plants cannot grow at temperatures below freezing. We can keep fruit from spoiling by keeping it frozen. What fruits are preserved this way?

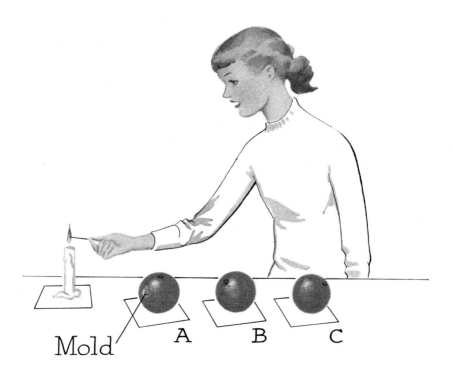

Mold A B C

Here is an experiment that will help you understand how bacteria are sometimes carried from one place to another. The experiment uses molds instead of bacteria because you can see the mold without a microscope.

Find an orange that has some mold growing on it. Push a needle into the mold and then prick a good orange with the needle. Now hold the needle in a candle flame for a moment to kill any mold on it. Then prick another good orange with the needle.

Mark the oranges and look at them a few days later.

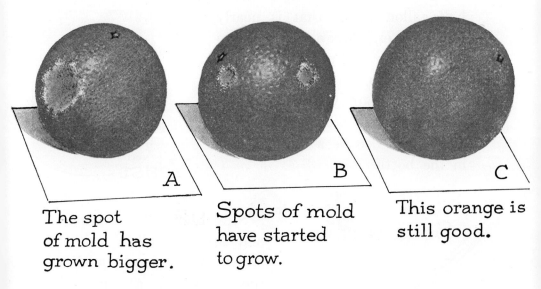

A

The spot
of mold has
grown bigger.

B

Spots of mold
have started
to grow.

C

This orange is
still good.

You will find mold growing on the first orange where
you pricked it. The other orange will not have mold
on it. Explain this.

Harmful bacteria may get into a cut in your skin
the same way. The things that cut you are not usually
clean. You can kill the bacteria in small cuts by
putting in chemicals called antiseptics. This should
be done before the bacteria begin to grow.

If possible, ask a doctor or a nurse to tell you how
to treat cuts to keep bacteria from growing in them.

Yeast

Put half a cup of sugar into a half gallon bottle that is nearly full of water. Mix a yeast cake in a little water and put some of it in the bottle too.

In a few hours you will see little bubbles rising from the water. There will also be a strange odor in the bottle.

Sugar water

Yeast

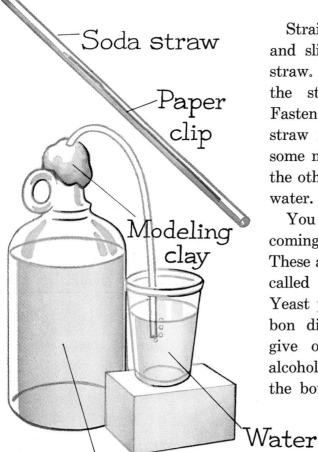

Soda straw

Paper clip

Modeling clay

Water

Sugar water and yeast

Straighten a paper clip and slip it inside a soda straw. You can now bend the straw in a curve. Fasten one end of the straw in the bottle with some modeling clay. Put the other end in a glass of water.

You will see bubbles coming from the straw. These are bubbles of a gas called **carbon dioxide.** Yeast plants give off carbon dioxide. They also give off alcohol. It is alcohol that you smell in the bottle.

22

Put a drop of the yeast mixture under a microscope. A toy microscope or a water-drop microscope will show you the little yeast plants. They look somewhat like the ones in the picture.

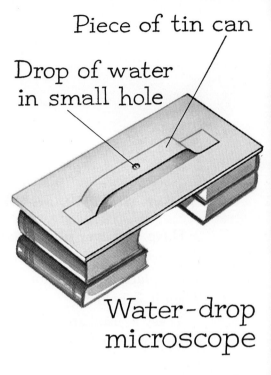

Piece of tin can

Drop of water in small hole

Water-drop microscope

Do any of the yeast plants have knobs growing on them. These knobs are called "buds." The buds grow rapidly if the yeast has plenty of food. The buds soon break off and become more yeast plants.

23

Buds

Newly mixed dough   Dough ready for baking

Yeast and Bread Making

Have you ever seen bread being made? The dough does not fill the pan at first. After it has been kept in a warm place for a few hours it swells up and fills the pan. Then it is baked.

Yeast is used to make the bread rise. You can try an experiment to show that yeast is needed to make it rise.

Find out from a cookbook how to make bread dough. Make some dough without any yeast in it. Make some more dough with yeast in it. Put some of both kinds of dough in glass dishes and set them in a warm place. Watch them and see what happens.

24

Dough
with
yeast

Dough
without
yeast

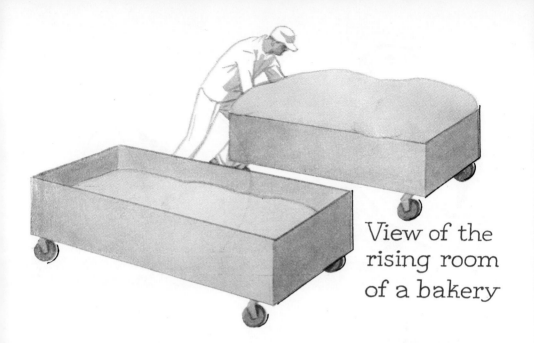

View of the
rising room
of a bakery

The yeast in the dough changes some of the starch into sugar. Then it uses the sugar for food. The yeast plants multiply very fast in the warm dough. Soon they give off bubbles of carbon dioxide.

These bubbles make the dough rise. When the dough is baked, the yeast is killed and the dough is cooked. The bread does not rise any more.

Look at a slice of bread. Notice the bubbles that were made by the carbon dioxide.

Try to visit a bakery to see bread being made.

Carbon dioxide
bubbles

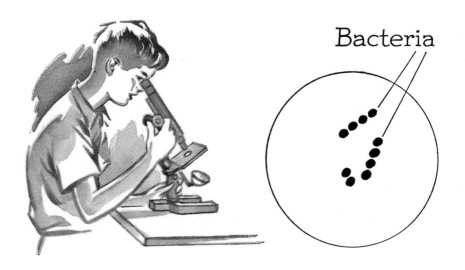

Bacteria

Bacteria

Bacteria are plants that are much smaller than yeasts and molds. You can see them only with a microscope.

Bacteria cannot make their own food. They must take their food from other things. Many bacteria are useful such as those that make the soil rich. Some kinds are harmful such as those that give off poisons and make people sick.

----

1. What can green plants do that other living things cannot do?
2. Where do mushrooms get their food?
3. What are the spores of mushrooms and molds?
4. Why is yeast put in bread?
5. How do yeast plants multiply?
6. What are some foods that are spoiled by mold and what are some foods that are made better?
7. Why does wood in damp places decay?

Saving the Soil

Topsoil

Subsoil

Topsoil and Subsoil

Dig into the soil of a field or a garden. If you cannot do this, visit a cellar or a roadway that has just been dug out.

You will see that the soil changes color a little below the top of the ground. The soil near the top is darker than the soil deeper down. The deeper soil is often yellow or red.

The upper soil is called **topsoil.** The lower soil is called **subsoil.** Usually the topsoil is less than two feet thick, although there are places where it is much thicker.

During heavy rains, streams of water may run down fields on steep hillsides. The streams pick up the topsoil and carry it away. Afterwards you may see gullies in the topsoil where the water has been flowing. Always it is the topsoil that is lost first.

We believe that we have lost a great deal of topsoil in this country since the forests were cut and the fields were first plowed. Some of it washed away. Some of it blew away.

It is said that a third of our topsoil is gone. There are a few places where little topsoil has been lost, but there are many places where it is all gone.

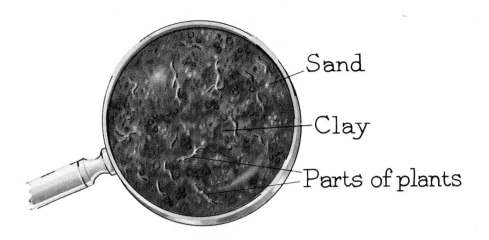

Sand

Clay

Parts of plants

What Is the Topsoil Like?

Look at some topsoil and some subsoil with a hand lens. What are some of the differences?

Topsoil has bits of dead plants in it. These bits of plants decay and become a dark material called **humus**. Humus gives topsoil its dark color.

Topsoil also has many living things in it. There are small animals. There are roots of plants. There are great numbers of tiny plants that are not green.

30

 Earthworm

 Millipede

Ant

Sow bug

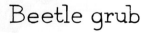
Beetle grub

Centipede

Plants usually grow best in loose soil. Their roots can push through it easily. They do not grow well in hard packed soil.

Break up some chunks of topsoil and subsoil with your fingers. Which chunks break apart more easily? Squeeze some wet topsoil and subsoil into balls and let them dry. Which break apart more easily?

Put some topsoil in one pan and some subsoil in another pan. Pour water into each until the water stands above the soil. Mix the water and soil and let them stand until they are dry. Which soil is harder when it dries? Which soil has more cracks in it?

These experiments show some of the reasons why topsoil is better for plants. Try planting seeds in both kinds of soil. Which plants grow better?

31

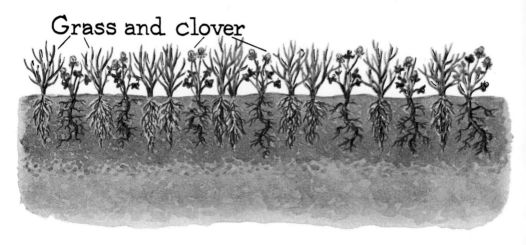

Grass and clover

Plants and Topsoil

Most plants grow well in topsoil. Topsoil is loose and the roots of plants push through it easily. Rain soaks into topsoil quickly. Topsoil usually has the minerals that plants need for good growth.

Topsoil is good for all kinds of cultivated crops. It is good for pastures. Good farms have thick topsoil.

If the topsoil is lost, most plants do not grow well. The subsoil is hard and it packs harder during every rain. The rain cannot soak in quickly. It either runs off or makes puddles on the soil.

Such land is almost worthless for cultivated crops and pastures. It becomes poorer every year unless something is done to make it into better soil.

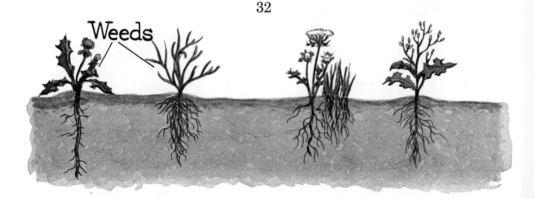

Weeds

Plants slowly change subsoil into topsoil if they are not disturbed. Their roots push into the subsoil, where they die and decay to form humus. Plants that are carried down into animal holes also change into humus. Humus from the top of the soil is washed down into holes in the subsoil.

Humus changes subsoil greatly. Get some humus from a woodland or buy some in a garden store. Add a little humus to some subsoil. How does the humus change the color of the subsoil? How does it change the way the subsoil packs together?

Punch holes in the bottoms of some metal cans and fill the cans with different mixtures of subsoil and humus. Pour equal amounts of water in each can and catch the water that runs through. How does humus change the amount of water that the soil soaks up?

Running Water and Topsoil

Running water carries away much of our topsoil. Whenever you see a muddy stream you are seeing valuable soil being carried away.

Bare hillsides lose topsoil very rapidly. During every rain, little streams of water begin to flow down the slopes. These little streams run together and make bigger streams. As the water rushes along, it picks up topsoil and carries it away. After one hard rain, a field may look like the one in the picture on this page.

Small gullies may not seem very bad. They are leveled off the next time the field is plowed. But we must never forget that valuable topsoil has been lost every time we see a gully, no matter how small.

After several rains, gullies may be so big that they cannot be plowed over. Then the field becomes useless. Unless something is done, the gullies grow deeper and longer. They may ruin other fields.

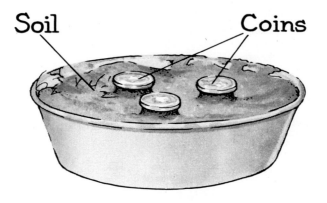

Soil　　　　　　　　Coins

Sheet Erosion

Fill a pan to the top with soil. Put two or three coins or flat stones on the soil. Set the pan outdoors on a rainy day. What happens?

If there is nothing to break the force of the raindrops, the soil is splashed about and mixed with water. As the water flows away, it takes some of the soil with it. A bare field loses some of its soil this way during every rain. This loss is called **sheet erosion.**

You can see signs of sheet erosion after heavy rains. Look for mud splashed on stones or plants. Look for stones held up by bits of soil while the soil around them has been washed away.

Not many people notice sheet erosion. There are no big gullies and there are no piles of mud at the bottom of a slope. Only a little soil is moved during one rain. Erosion is slow.

But year after year, sheet erosion goes on. A field loses more topsoil than it gets back. In time, so much topsoil has been lost that the field becomes worthless.

This picture shows a field that has lost nearly all its topsoil by sheet erosion. Perhaps you can find a field like this. Many farms have been made worthless by sheet erosion.

37

Destroying the Soil Cover

Plants are the best protectors of the topsoil. When we kill plants we increase the loss of our topsoil.

Of course, we must kill plants when we want to raise a crop. We must plow the wild plants under and leave the field bare for a time. However, it is safer to plow some fields than others. Steep hillsides should not be plowed. Why is it safe to plow level fields?

People often kill plants by being careless or thoughtless. Some people start grass fires without thinking that the fire kills many of the plants and burns up much of the humus in the soil. Grass fires increase the loss of topsoil.

38

People often make the mistake of keeping too many sheep or cattle in one field. The animals eat the plants off close to the ground trying to find enough to eat. Soon the plants die and the topsoil begins to wash away. This picture shows a field which has become worthless, and these cattle can not be kept here.

Forest Fires and Topsoil

Forest fires not only destroy many trees each year, but they also cause the loss of much topsoil. Trees are good cover for the soil. Their roots hold it tightly. The leaves and twigs that they drop help stop sheet erosion. Humus comes from the leaves and other parts of the trees as they decay.

The picture shows us what happens in a forest fire. The leaves and twigs are burning. Small trees are being killed. The humus in the top layer of soil is being destroyed.

A hillside may look like this after a forest fire. There is nothing to hold the soil. Rain is already beginning to wash the soil away. The hillside may come to look like the picture below before new plants can grow and protect the soil.

41

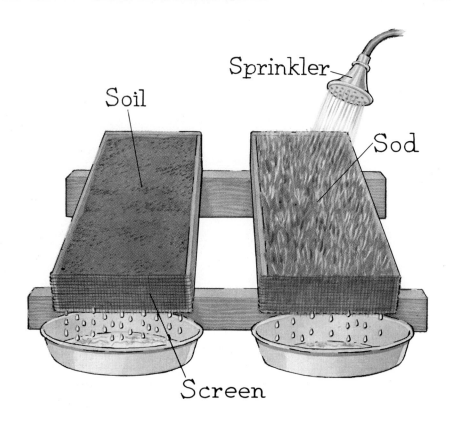

Soil

Sprinkler

Sod

Screen

Giving Soil a New Cover

Make two trays like the ones shown above. The trays should be about three feet long. One end of each tray is closed with a board, and the other end has a piece of metal screening tacked across it.

Fill one tray with fine soil. Fill the other with fine soil covered by sod. Put blocks under the trays so they will slope.

Sprinkle each tray with the same amount of water. Catch the water that comes from the low end of each tray. Which tray loses more water? Which tray loses more soil?

The picture above shows poor soil. Only a little grass and a few weeds are growing there. These plants help hold the soil, but there are many open places where there can be sheet erosion. If the slope were steep enough, gullies might start in this field.

We can give this field a good cover of plants by fertilizing and seeding it with clover and grasses. The field will then become a good pasture instead of a worthless piece of land.

43

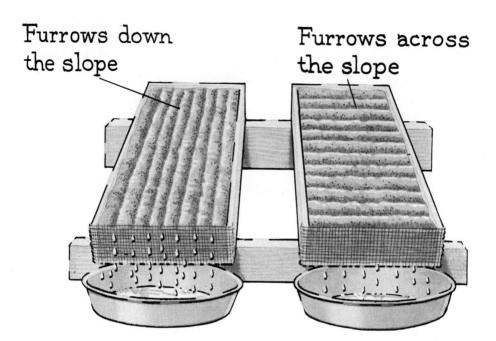

Furrows down the slope

Furrows across the slope

Contour Plowing

We must plow fields in order to have cultivated crops. We should learn to plow fields carefully so that not much soil is lost.

Use the same trays that you used in the last experiment. Fill each tray with fine soil. Put a block under each tray so that the slope of each is the same. Use a stick to make furrows up and down the slope in one tray and across the slope in the other tray. Sprinkle each tray with the same amount of water and catch the water that drips out.

Which tray loses more water? Which tray loses more soil? Explain why.

44

In the picture above we see a field that has been plowed up and down the slope. See how rain has made gullies in it. Explain why.

Below we see a farmer plowing along the slope. His furrows are level. His furrows curve where the hill curves. This is called **contour plowing** because the furrows follow a level line around the hill.

Why is contour plowing helpful in saving the soil? Why will soil be lost even with contour plowing?

45

Strip Cropping and Crop Rotation

Even with careful plowing, gullies may start in a large, sloping field during a heavy rain. Little streams join together and make streams big enough to dig deep gullies.

Wise farmers use **strip cropping** with their contour plowing. They raise different crops in strips along the slopes. The picture shows strip cropping on a hillside.

There is a pasture at the bottom of the hill at the right side of the picture. Above that there is a strip of potatoes. Then comes a strip of grass that will be cut for hay. Above that are strips of winter wheat, corn, and more winter wheat. At the top there is grass for hay.

If a gully starts in one strip, the plants in the next strip stop it before it becomes very big. Soil may wash down the slope a short way, but it is soon stopped.

It is not wise to plant the same crop in a field year after year. Each kind of crop needs certain minerals from the soil, and it will quickly use up the minerals if nothing else is planted. The humus in the soil disappears, too, if nothing is done to put some humus back into the soil.

A wise farmer changes his crops around each year. He may plant potatoes this year where he planted wheat last year. He may plant corn next year where he grew hay this year. He will also plant things that can be plowed under to make humus.

It is helpful to plant clover or one of its relatives every few years. There are useful bacteria that live on the roots of the clover family. These bacteria can take gases from the air and change them into minerals that plants need for good growth.

47

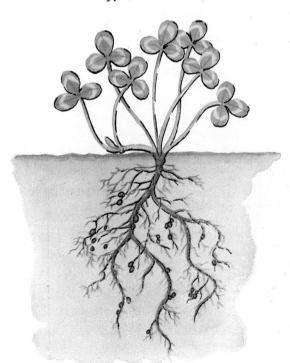

Ways of Stopping Gullies

Gullies should be stopped before they grow long and ruin nearby fields. A field with many deep gullies in it may never again be good for cultivated crops.

The gullies in the upper picture were kept from growing longer by planting vines and other plants along the banks. Four years later the gullies looked like the picture below.

48

Dig gullies with fingers

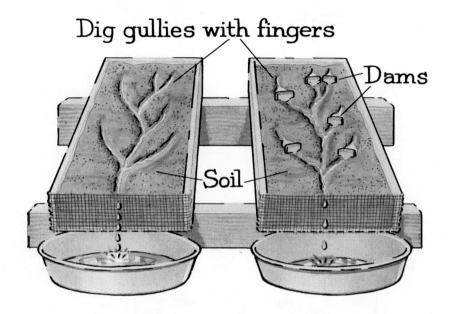

Dams

Soil

Sometimes gullies are too big to be stopped with trash and vines. Then dams should be built across the gullies. The dams slow down the water so that it does not dig into the soil so rapidly.

Set up an experiment to show how dams help slow down the water in gullies.

Conservation NOT at work. UNWISE use of natural resources.

Conservation AT work. WISE use of natural resources.

New York State Conservation Department

Wind Erosion

This is a picture of a dust storm. Much topsoil can be lost in storms of this kind. The dust usually comes from bare fields. How can this loss be kept smaller?

---

1. What is topsoil?
2. How does subsoil become topsoil?
3. What are some reasons why topsoil is lost?
4. How do grass fires and forest fires harm the soil?
5. What is contour plowing and why is it used?
6. How can we keep topsoil on steep hillsides?
7. What can we do to keep gullies from becoming bigger?

Time and Seasons

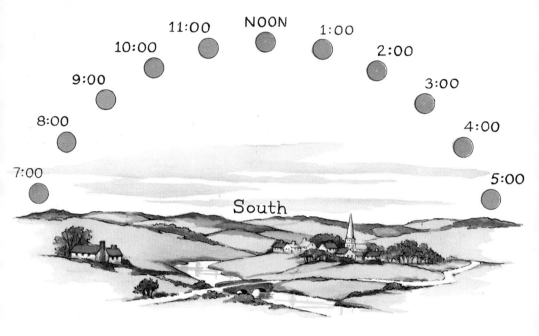

11:00   NOON   1:00
10:00   2:00
9:00   3:00
8:00   4:00
7:00   5:00

South

The Sun and Its Shadows

Every day the sun seems to rise, to move across the sky, and to set again. It is so regular in its movements that it has always been a good timekeeper.

Today we have clocks to help us tell time, but we still use the sun also. We know the difference between morning and afternoon by the sun. We know when evening is near at hand. We know when it is nearly noon.

You will find the sun very useful as a timekeeper. Make a habit of noticing where it is at different times of day. Often you will be able to guess the time when you have no watch.

Drive a pole into the ground in a place that is sunny all day. Watch the shadow of the pole. How does it change as the sun moves?

Each hour drive a small stake into the ground at the end of the shadow of the pole. Mark each stake so that you can tell when you drove it into the ground. You can use the stakes to tell time for several days.

Use a compass to find the direction the shadows point. Find the shadow that points most nearly north.

Days, Years, and Months

Until about 500 years ago, people believed that the sun travelled around the earth. They said that a day was the time needed for the sun to go once around the earth.

Today we believe that the earth is round and that it spins like a top. We also believe that the earth travels around the sun.

We say that a day is the time needed for the earth to turn around once. Put a globe in sunlight and turn it slowly. When the sun is over the place where you live, it is noon. Turn the globe until it is noon again. One day has passed.

Sunlight

Let us suppose that the earth is really spinning as most people believe. Then the reason that the sun seems to move across the sky is because we ourselves are moving.

Go outdoors and look at the sky. Which way does the sun seem to move? Which way must the earth be spinning to make the sun seem to move as it does?

Look at the skyline in the west. Imagine that it is rising. What will happen when the skyline reaches the sun?

Look at the eastern skyline and imagine that it is moving. When does sunrise come?

Where will you be when midnight comes?

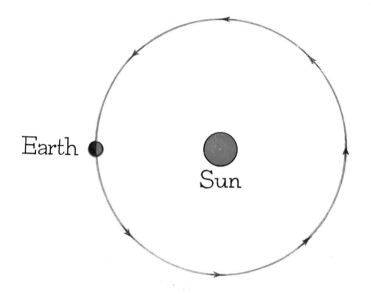

Earth

Sun

We believe that the earth has another motion too. We believe that it travels around the sun in a path that is almost a circle. The time needed for the earth to travel once around the sun is called a year.

The earth needs about 365¼ days to travel once around the sun. When we divide the year into days, there is a quarter of a day left over. We cannot put a quarter of a day on the calendar, so we add one full day every four years. In what month do we add the extra day? When will the extra day be added again?

FEBRUARY						
S	M	T	W	T	F	S
					1	2
3	4	5	6	7	8	9
10	11	12	13	14	15	16
17	18	19	20	21	22	23
24	25	26	27	28	29	

Crescent   First Quarter   Full Moon   Last Quarter   Crescent

The word "month" comes from the same word that gives us the word "moon." A month has often been called a "moon."

Watch the moon for a few weeks and you will see that it changes shape. At first it is a little sliver of light in the western sky. Night by night it grows larger until it is fully round. Then it grows smaller again until you can no longer see it.

The time needed for the moon to go through these changes is almost 30 days. There are twelve "moons" in a year with a few days left over. Count the days in each month to see how we take care of the extra days.

JANUARY						
S	M	T	W	T	F	S
		1	2	3	4	5
6	7	8	9	10	11	12
13	14	15	16	17	18	19
20	21	22	23	24	25	26
27	28	29	30	31		

Sundial

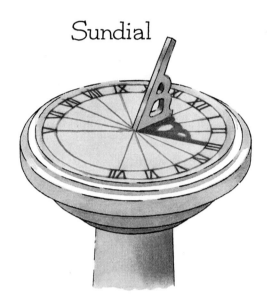

Twelve-hour clock

Clock Faces

When the sundial was invented, people decided to divide the time of daylight into twelve parts called hours. Later, they decided to divide the whole day into two parts of twelve hours each. That is why we now have clocks that show only twelve hours even though the day is twenty-four hours long.

How many times in one day does the hour hand of the clock shown above go around? Does the clock tell you whether it is day or night? How do you know whether it is day or night?

How do we write time so that it tells whether it is before or after noon? Look at some timetables and find out how to tell whether a train or a bus leaves in the daytime or the nighttime.

60

The twelve-hour clock often causes trouble. A person may miss a train if he makes a mistake in reading a timetable. Sometimes a person writes down the time and forgets to write A.M. or P.M. after it, and then he does not know what the time really should be.

The twenty-four-hour clock is easier to use. The hour hand goes around once a day. 1200 hours is noon. 600 hours is the same as 6:00 A.M. 1800 hours is the same as 6:00 P.M. What time is 1500 hours?

The armed forces of some countries use the twenty-four hour clock. How can a mistake between A.M. and P.M. be important to an army or navy?

Make a clock face with twenty-four hours on it. Fasten on hands that will turn around. Keep the hands set at the proper time.

61

Twenty-four-hour clock

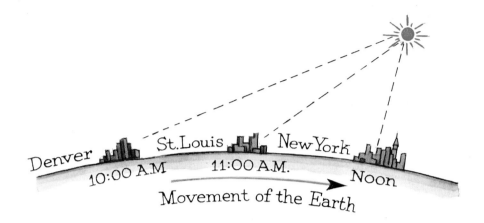

Denver St. Louis New York
10:00 A.M. 11:00 A.M. Noon
Movement of the Earth

Time Over the Earth

When using a radio or a television set, have you noticed that football games in one part of the country do not come at the same times as they would where you live? Many places in the country have a time different from your own. Listen to a radio or watch television, and keep a record of places that have different times.

The diagrams on this page show why we have different time in different places. The sun cannot be overhead everywhere at the same time, so noon must come earlier in some places than in others. When it is noon in New York City, people in St. Louis must wait about an hour before noon comes. Look at these diagrams and explain the difference in time in the other cities.

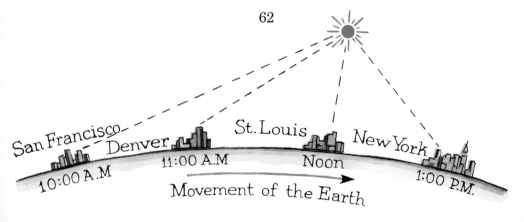

San Francisco Denver St. Louis New York
10:00 A.M 11:00 A.M Noon 1:00 P.M.
Movement of the Earth

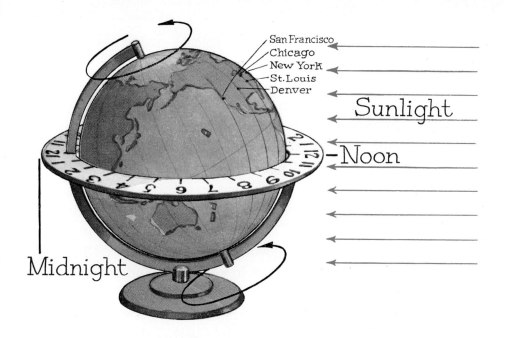

San Francisco
Chicago
New York
St. Louis
Denver

Sunlight

Noon

Midnight

This picture shows how time changes over the whole earth. Imagine that the earth is turning inside the ring. It is noon in New York and the sun is overhead. What time is it in San Francisco? In Shanghai? In what part of the world is it midnight?

Set a globe in sunlight and turn it until it is like this picture. Where is the sunrise? Where is the sunset?

From the picture above, you can see that the earth must turn for three hours before it is noon in San Francisco. Turn the globe until it is noon in San Francisco. Where is the sunrise now? Where is the sunset? Where is it midnight? Can you figure out what time it is in Chicago?

Turn the globe until it is midnight in San Francisco. How many hours would the earth have needed to turn half way around like this? Where is it noon?

Standard Time

Once every city had its own time. What would happen as you went from one place to another? What do you think a timetable would look like? Give some reasons why we would not like so many kinds of time today.

When railroads became common it was decided to have fewer kinds of time. The country was divided into four time zones as are shown on the map below. The time is the same everywhere in each zone and is called standard time. Which time zone do you live in?

Study some train, bus, and airplane timetables. Pretend that you are taking a trip across the country. Where would you change your watch? How would you change it?

64

Bring four clocks to school and start them running. Set one clock to read the time in your own time zone. Set the other clocks to read the time in each of the other time zones of the country.

Imagine what is going on in schools in other time zones. When you are eating lunch what are the other pupils doing? When you leave school, are other pupils still in school or did they go home earlier? When you are starting school what are the other pupils doing?

Some cities and towns move the clock ahead one hour during the summer months. This is called daylight saving time.

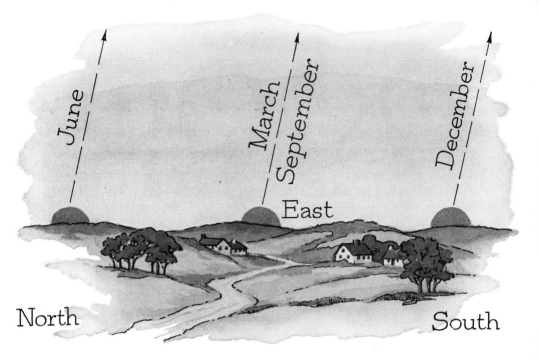

The Changing Path of the Sun

People sometimes say that the sun rises in the east and sets in the west. Let us see if this is always true.

Watch the sun rise in the morning and make a note of the place where you first saw it. A good way of keeping a record is by making a drawing like the one above. Keep a record of the time too.

Use a compass to find out if the sun came up exactly in the east.

A few days later watch the sun come up again. Does it come up in the same place as it did before? Is it farther to the north or to the south? Did the time change?

Find out whether the sun sets in the west the same way. Find out whether the time of sunset changes. Make records of the time and place on a drawing of the western skyline.

If you like this kind of science work, keep a record of sunrise and sunset for several months.

An almanac gives the time of sunrise and sunset. Which day has the earliest sunrise? Which day has the latest sunset? Which day has the latest sunrise? Which day has the earliest sunset?

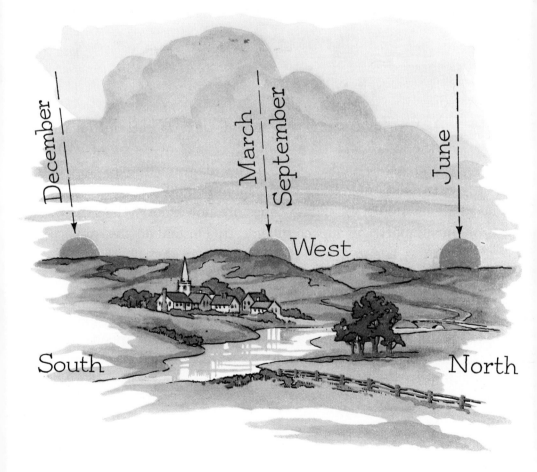

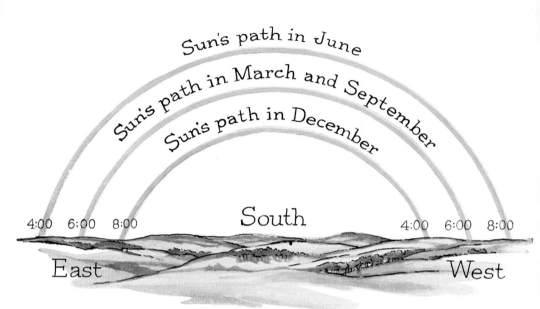

Sun's path in June

Sun's path in March and September

Sun's path in December

4:00 6:00 8:00   South   4:00 6:00 8:00

East   West

If we could watch the sun all day on certain days
of the year, and then make drawings of its path, we
would have something like the diagram above.

In December the sun rises about 8:00 A.M. and sets
about 4:00 P.M. These times are not exactly the same
in all parts of the country. In December the sun's
path is a curve low in the southern sky.

During the next few months, the days become longer
and the sun's path becomes higher. In March there
are a few days when the daylight hours and the night
hours are about the same in length. What happens to
the length of the daylight hours between March and
June? What happens between June and December?

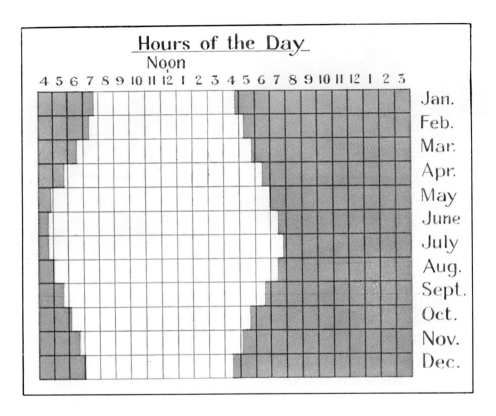

Hours of the Day

Noon

4 5 6 7 8 9 10 11 12 1 2 3 4 5 6 7 8 9 10 11 12 1 2 3

Jan.
Feb.
Mar.
Apr.
May
June
July
Aug.
Sept.
Oct.
Nov.
Dec.

Above is a record of the hours of daylight and darkness in Washington, D. C. The record would be a little different for other cities.

Make a record like this for your own city or town. You can find the times of sunrise and sunset in an almanac.

Count the hours of daylight in one day of each month. Which one has the most daylight? Which has the least daylight? Which days have nearly equal hours of daylight and darkness?

Noon
June 21

In late June the sun is almost overhead every noon. In December the sun is low in the southern sky at noon.

What do the shadows in these two pictures tell you about the position of the sun in the sky? Once a month make a picture record of the shadows around your school.

Noon
December 21

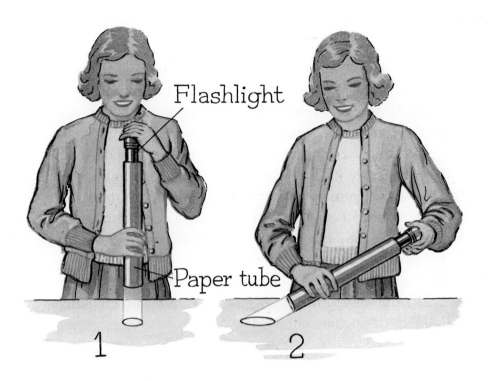

Flashlight

Paper tube

1   2

Make a roll of heavy paper to fit around a flashlight as shown in the pictures above. Darken the room as much as possible and turn on the flashlight.

First hold the tube straight up and down. Then slant the tube slowly. What happens to the spot of light? When is the spot brightest?

In summer at noon the sun shines almost straight down as the flashlight does in the first picture. In winter at noon the sun shines on a greater slant as the flashlight does in the second picture. Which is brighter, winter sunlight or summer sunlight?

71

Seasons and Weather

You should now know about the two reasons why summers are warmer than winters. 1) Summer sunshine is warmer than winter sunshine. 2) The sun shines longer in summer than in winter.

In summer the soil, the water, and the air gain more heat than they lose. In winter they lose more heat than they gain. Put some dry soil in one pan and some water in another pan. Place a thermometer in each pan. Set the two pans in sunlight and read the temperatures every ten minutes. Now place the pans in shade and read the temperatures every ten minutes.

Do the temperatures of the soil and water change quickly or do they change slowly?

72

Water   Soil

This experiment should help you understand several things about the weather. The sun is warmest at noon but the warmest part of the day is usually later in the afternoon. This is because the soil, water, and air heat up slowly. The coldest part of the day is often just before sunrise. This is because the soil, water, and air cool slowly.

Sunlight is warmest in late June. Why are July and August usually the warmest months?

Heating and cooling in one place may change the weather for people many miles away. During the winter in central Canada, the air may cool to 50 degrees below zero. Masses of this cold air break away and move south over the United States. They bring very cold weather with them. Watch some weather maps this winter to see how far some cold masses move.

There is warm air over the Gulf of Mexico, too. Masses of this warm air often move north and bring warm weather. Watch weather maps for these masses.

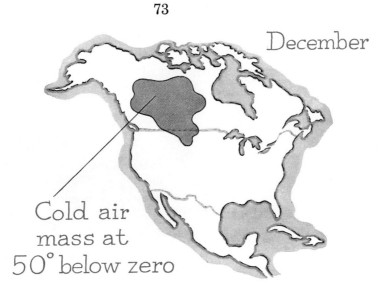

December

Cold air
mass at
50° below zero

Spring

Fall

The Seasons and Living Things

Many living things change as the seasons change. Some plants grow new leaves in spring and lose them in the fall. Name some plants that lose their leaves in the fall, and name some that do not lose them. Some plants, such as tulips, bloom only in the spring. Others, such as goldenrod, bloom only in late summer and fall. Some plants, such as petunias, bloom all summer. Name more plants of each kind.

Experiments show that a change in the amount of light changes the way some plants grow. Greenhouse workers have learned that some plants bloom only when the days are long. They make these plants bloom in winter by turning on electric lights for a few hours each evening. They have learned that other plants bloom only when the days are short. They make these plants bloom in summer by covering them with a dark cloth part of each day. Visit a greenhouse and ask about these plants.

74

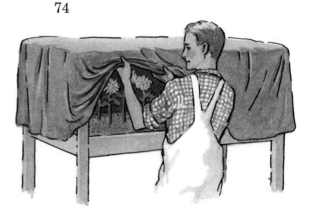

Chrysanthemum
a short day flower

Goldfinch in winter

Goldfinch in summer

Insects, toads, snakes, and many other animals are more active in warm weather than in cold weather. Most of them crawl into hiding places in the fall and are quiet until warm weather comes again.

However, woodchucks of the northeastern states begin their winter sleep in late summer and end it in late winter. It cannot be temperature that makes them do this. We do not know the real cause.

Many birds also fly south in late summer while the weather is still warm. Some experiments make us think that the change in the length of day sends them south, but we do not know for sure.

It is also interesting to study the way animals change their coats as the seasons change. Most birds and fur-bearing animals lose their old coats in late summer. Some of them also gain new coats in early spring as well. We do not know what makes them do this. There is much for us to learn about animals.

75

Weasel in winter

Weasel in summer

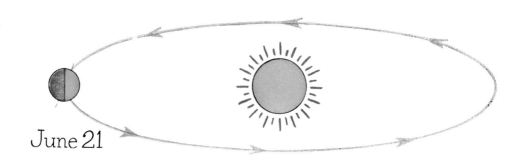

June 21

Why Seasons Change

We have seen that long daylight hours and a sun high in the sky bring warmer weather. Let us now see why the sun's path changes.

We believe that the earth goes around the sun along a path that is almost a circle. We also believe that the earth is tipped a little as shown in the pictures on this page.

In June the northern half is tipped toward the sun. This part of the earth has more sunlight in June than at other times of the year. The land, the water, and the air become warm.

76

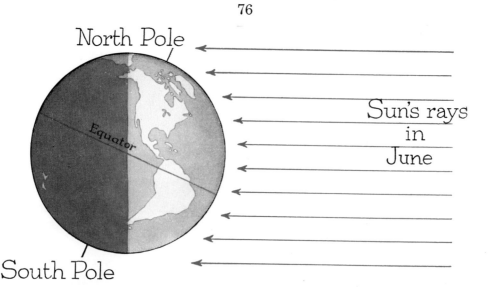

North Pole

Equator

South Pole

Sun's rays in June

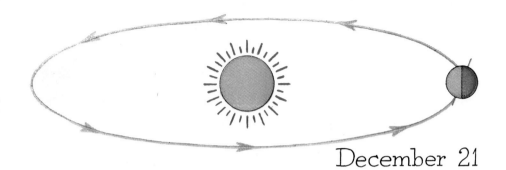

December 21

As the earth moves along its path, it is always tipped the same way. By December, when the earth is on the other side of the sun, the northern half is tipped away from the sun.

Now the nights in the north are long and the sun's path is low in the sky. This part of the earth loses more heat than it gets from the sun each day. Winter comes.

When does summer come to the southern part of the earth? When does winter come?

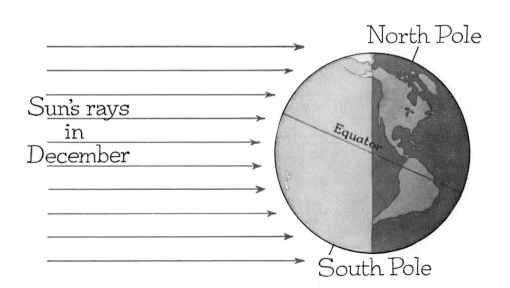

North Pole

Sun's rays
in
December

Equator

South Pole

A model like the one above may help you understand the change of seasons. Use a lamp in the center of a large table for the sun. Use apples or small globes to show where the earth is during each of the four seasons.

In which season does sunlight fall most directly on the northern part of the earth? When does it fall most directly on the southern part? When does it fall equally on the two parts of the earth?

—Rubber band

—Wire

Pretend that a lamp is the sun. Carry a globe around the lamp. Always keep the globe tipped in the same direction. Turn the globe slowly so that there is day and night on the globe.

Notice the changes in the length of the daylight hours in different parts of the globe as you carry it around the sun.

79

This is a scene in Australia on January first. Explain why people can go swimming there on New Year's Day.

In what other parts of the world does summer come in late December?

---

1. What motion of the earth gives us day and night?
2. What is an hour?
3. Why does noon come at different times across the United States?
4. What is standard time?
5. Why are summers warmer than winters?
6. What causes the change of seasons?
7. What are some plants and animals that change with the seasons?

Our Eyes

 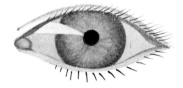

Studying Our Eyes

The first thing you may notice about eyes is their color. What color are your eyes? What colors are the eyes of your classmates? What is the most common eye color in your class?

Try to find out the color of the eyes of your parents and grandparents. Are your eyes like any of theirs? Which of your classmates have eyes like their parents' and grandparents'?

Do any of your pets have eyes somewhat like yours? What are the colors of their eyes?

82

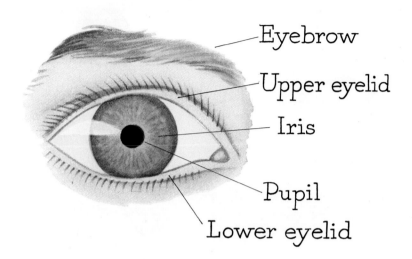

Eyebrow

Upper eyelid

Iris

Pupil

Lower eyelid

Look closely at some of the parts of an eye. The colored part is called the **iris.** The black part in the center of the iris is called the **pupil.**

The pupil is an opening in the iris. The pupil looks black because the inside of the eye is dark. Light reflected from things around us goes into the eye through the pupil.

There is a clear covering over the front of the eye. Look at someone's eye from the side and you will see the clear covering.

83

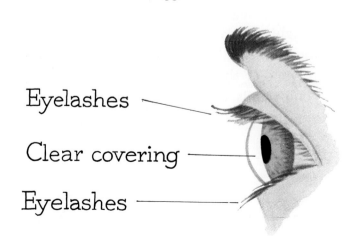

Eyelashes

Clear covering

Eyelashes

The Iris and the Pupil

Sit so that you and a classmate can look into each other's eyes. Close your eyes and cover them with your hands. Your classmate should do the same. At the end of one minute your teacher will say "Time." Then look at the pupils of your classmate's eyes. What happens?

Pupils can change in size. They are small when the light is bright. They are large when the light is dim. When you go into a bright place, your pupils close and keep out some of the light. When you go into a dark place, your pupils open and let in as much light as possible.

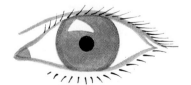

Have you noticed what happens when you go into a dark theater on a sunny afternoon? At first you cannot see your way to a seat. After a few minutes you can see your way. Your pupils have opened and let in more light.

Do your eyes hurt when you turn on a bright light after being in a dark room? Your pupils are large in the dark room. They let in so much bright light that your eyes hurt. After a few minutes, however, you can see better and your eyes are comfortable. What happens?

85

How Our Eyes Are Protected

Press the back of your hand against your eye. What keeps your hand from hurting your eye?

Look at the drawings of the skull. Notice how well your eyes are protected by the bones around them. The eyes fit into hollows in the skull, and bones make a ring around each eye.

Touch your face with your fingers. Find the forehead bones. Find the nose bone. Find the cheek bones.

86

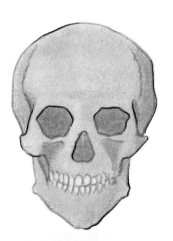
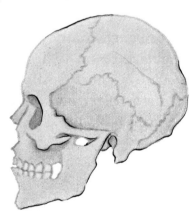

The bones around your eyes cannot keep small or sharp things from hurting your eyes. You must learn to be careful with such things.

Make up some rules for doing the following:
1. Handing a knife to someone else.
2. Cutting a string with a knife.
3. Whittling a stick.
4. Lighting matches.
5. Pretending to fight with sticks.
6. Running with a stick in your hand.

Make up some other rules that will help you protect your eyes.

Suppose that you are in a pillow fight and a pillow is thrown at your face. What are some of the things you do to keep your eyes from being hit? Which of these things do you do without thinking about them?

Do you usually blink your eyes when something flies toward them? Do you think about blinking your eyes or do they seem to close by themselves?

We do many things without thinking about them. Watch someone's eyes when he does not know you are looking. Does he blink his eyes? Do you know of other things people do without thinking?

Look at the hair growing around someone's eyes. There is an eyebrow over each eye. Some people think that eyebrows help keep sweat from running into the eyes on hot days. Eyebrows might also keep rain from running down into the eyes.

The hairs on your eyelids are called eyelashes. Eyelashes help keep dust from your eyes when the wind is blowing. You can nearly close your eyes and look through the eyelashes. The eyelashes make a screen that helps keep out dust.

Ask someone to nearly close his eyes. Notice how the eyelashes fit together.

89

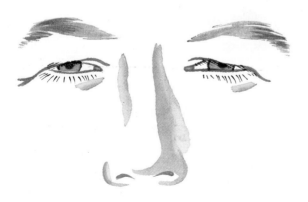

Tears

There are tears in your eyes all the time. A gland near the outer corner of each eye is always making tears. The tears flow across your eyes as you blink. Then the tears run into small holes to your nose.

Look at your eyes in a mirror. You will see the two small holes in the inside corner of each eye.

Tears keep your eyes from drying out. They also wash dust from your eyes.

Sometimes you make a great many tears. Where do they go? Do you know why you must blow your nose when you cry?

90

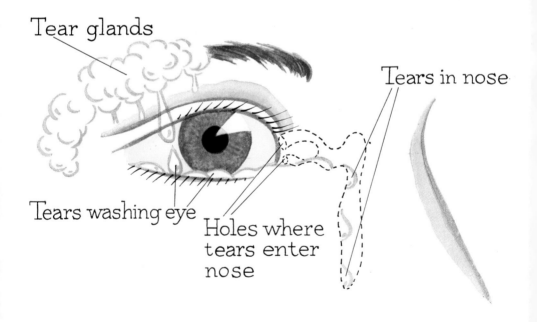

Tear glands

Tears in nose

Tears washing eye

Holes where tears enter nose

Removing Dirt

Many tears come into your eyes when you get a bit of dirt in them. How does crying help take out the dirt?

You should not rub your eyes when there is dirt in them. The dirt may be sharp and you will scratch the inside of the eyelid or the eyeball.

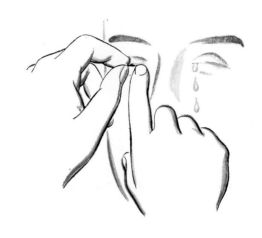

It is often easy to take out a bit of dirt that gets under the upper eyelid. Take hold of the upper eyelashes and pull the upper eyelid out over the lower lid. Then let it slide back over the lower lid. The lower eyelashes will often brush off the bit of dirt.

Sometimes you will need help in taking dirt from your eyes. A doctor or a nurse knows best how to do this.

91

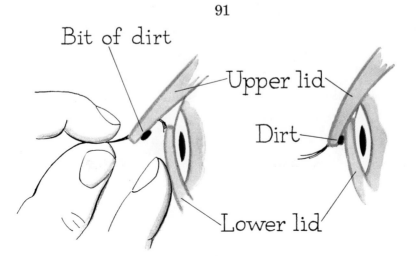

Bit of dirt

Upper lid

Dirt

Lower lid

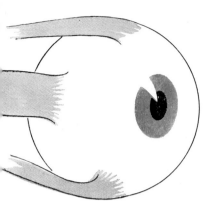

Moving the Eyes

An eye is shaped much like a ball. You can see only a small part of the eye between the eyelids. The rest of it is hidden inside the head.

Watch someone moving his eyes. Move your own eyes from side to side and up and down. Move a pencil upwards. How far can you watch it without moving your head? Move the pencil to one side and then the other. How far can you watch it without turning your head?

There are muscles fastened to each eyeball. Three muscles are shown in the picture on this page. These muscles turn the eyeball so you can look in different directions without turning your head.

Your eye muscles also turn your eyes toward each other when you look at something close. When you look at something far away, the muscles turn your eyes until they both look straight ahead.

Face a window and hold a pencil at arm's length. Look just over the pencil at a pole or a tree outside the window. How many pencils do you see? Now look at the pencil. How many poles do you see?

When you look at the pole, neither eye is turned toward the pencil. You see two pencils, one with each eye, in different places. When you look at the pencil, both eyes turn toward it and you see only one pencil.

Watch someone's eyes as he does this experiment.

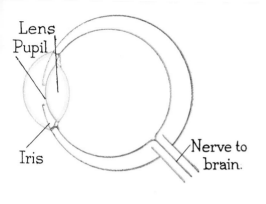

Lens
Pupil
Iris
Nerve to brain.

The Lens in the Eye

There is a lens inside each eyeball. It is just behind the pupil. The lens has the shape of a magnifying lens.

An experiment with a magnifying lens will show what the lens in your eye does. Stand with your back to a window. Hold the lens in front of a sheet of paper and move it backwards and forwards. You will be able to make a picture of the window on the sheet of paper.

The lens in your eye makes a picture on the back of the eyeball. There are many nerves in this part of the eyeball. The nerves lead to your brain and let you know what you see.

94

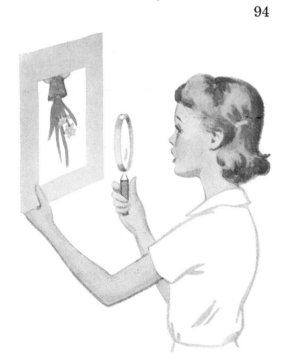

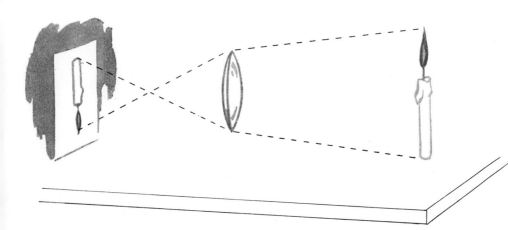

The lens in your eye is unlike a glass lens in one important way. You can make the lens in your eye thicker or thinner.

This experiment shows what thick lenses and thin lenses can do. You will need two lenses, one much thicker than the other. Set up the materials shown above and darken the room. Move the candle back and forth until its picture shows on the paper.

Then change the lenses. Hold the second lens in the same place that you held the first lens. Move the candle back and forth until its picture shows on the paper.

The thick lens makes a picture when the candle is close to the paper. The thin lens makes a picture when the candle is farther away.

Changing the Shape of the Lens of the Eye

Shut one eye and hold a pencil near the other eye. Look first at the pencil. Then look at something far away. Sometimes you will feel a change inside your eye as you look from one thing to another. You are making the lens in your eye thicker and thinner.

Can you see the pencil clearly when you are looking at something far away? Can you see far away things clearly when you are looking at the pencil?

There are muscles around the lens in the eye. The muscles can make the lens thicker. The closer the things that you are looking at, the thicker the muscles make the lens.

96

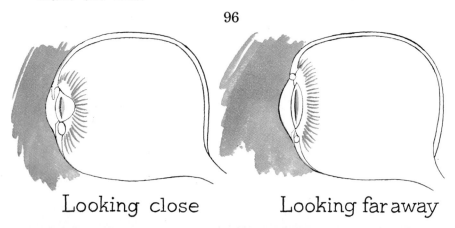

Looking close   Looking far away

Some people have eye muscles that do not work perfectly. If they cannot make the lenses in their eyes thin enough, they cannot see distant things clearly. These people are "nearsighted." If they cannot make the lenses in their eyes thick enough, they cannot see nearby things clearly. These people are "farsighted."

Such people need glasses. The lenses in the glasses help such people see more clearly.

Every person should have his eyes tested by a doctor. The doctor can tell whether the person needs glasses. He will also look for diseases or injuries to the eyes and treat any that he finds.

97

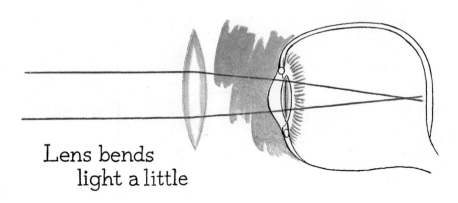

Lens bends
light a little

Good Light for Seeing

Lens muscles must work hardest when you are looking at things close to you. Therefore you should be most careful when you are reading or doing close work.

You should not read or do close work too long at one time. Rest your eyes if you can by going outdoors to work or play. If you cannot go outdoors try to do some other kind of work.

Try to have a good light when you read or do close work. The best light is outdoors in the shade of a house or a tree. But do not let sunlight fall on your book because it will reflect into your eyes.

At night use several lights in different parts of the room. Then you will have a strong light on your work and there will not be many shadows.

When you read sit so that the strongest light comes over your shoulder. Then the light will not reflect from the book into your eyes.

Try not to have shadows on your work. If you are right-handed it is usually better to have the light come from your left side.

You should not read when you are sick. Your eyes then need a rest just as other parts of your body do.

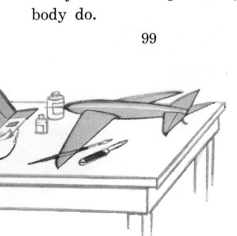

Rabbit

Animal Eyes

Many animals have eyes somewhat like our own, although there are usually many differences, too.

A rabbit's eyes are placed at the sides of its head. The rabbit can see nearly all the way around without turning its head. How does this help the rabbit?

The eyes of a meadow mouse are near the top of its head. How does this help the meadow mouse?

Where are our eyes? Where are the eyes of a cat, a robin, a squirrel, an owl, and a frog?

100

Frog

Meadow mouse

Bass

Look at the eyes of a goldfish or some other fish. Does the fish have eyelids? Does it close its eyes? Can it move its eyes?

Have you noticed that you cannot see clearly when you are under water? Probably a fish cannot see clearly when it is in the air. The eye lenses of animals that live in the water are usually thicker than the eye lenses of animals that live in the air.

Fish that live in dark, muddy water, such as catfish, may have small eyes. They seem to find their food by smell or taste rather than by sight. Fish that hunt living animals usually have large eyes.

There are a few kinds of fish that live in caves where there is no light. These fish are often blind. They have eyes, but their eyes are useless.

Catfish

Eyes of Animals at Night

Animals that are active at night often have large eyes. The pupils of their eyes become very large in the dark. How may this be of help to the animals?

Study a cat's eyes. Notice the pupils on a bright day. What shape are the pupils? Put the cat in a room where the light is dim. What happens to the pupils?

Name some other animals that are active at night. Which ones have large eyes?

Have you ever seen a pair of eyes shining along the road at night? Did you see the animal?

Some people think that such eyes give off light much as a flashlight does. You will see these eyes shining, however, only when the animal is facing a bright light. The light reflects from a layer in the back of the animal's eyes. You see reflected light.

What colors have you seen reflected by animals' eyes at night?

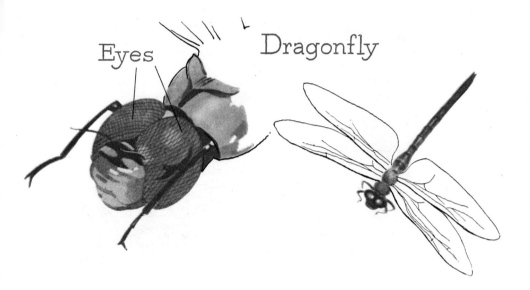

Eyes

Dragonfly

Insects have eyes that are much different from our own. Many insects have more than two eyes. Often two of their eyes are made up of hundreds of tiny prisms. We are not certain just how things look through all these prisms, but we do know that some of these insects have good sight.

1. Where does light enter the eye?
2. What is the shape of the lens in an eye?
3. What are some ways our eyes are protected from being hit?
4. What happens to your eyes as you go from a dark place to a brightly lighted place?
5. Why are your eyes under greatest strain when you read or do close work?
6. List some rules for the care of the eyes.
7. Name some animals that can see well at night.

Making Work Easier

Dividing Work

Suppose that you must move a large pile of bricks. You are not strong enough to lift the whole pile at once. What would you do?

How could a small child move the pile of bricks? How could a strong man move them? Who would do the work faster?

Here we see an important way for doing work more easily. We can divide work into small parts and do one part at a time. We do the same amount of work but we do it more easily. We lose speed as we make work easier.

This man is dividing his work into small parts. He is moving a pile of dirt one shovelful at a time. He will stop filling the wheelbarrow before it becomes too heavy to move easily.

How could a small boy move the pile of dirt?

Make a list of other kinds of work that we can do more easily by dividing each into small parts.

We can often use our minds to help us do something more easily. We look for ways of doing the work more slowly. We can save in force by giving up speed.

Using a Slope

Find a long board and a short board. Put one end of the short board on a box.

Fill a gallon jar or a round can with sand. Lift it straight up. Roll it up the short board. Roll it up the long board. Is it easier to lift the jar straight up or roll it up a board? Which board made the work easier?

This experiment shows a way to make work easier. We use less force when we roll the jar up the long board. We need less force when we do work more slowly.

These men have found a way to move some heavy boxes into the truck. They are pushing the boxes up a long plank. By moving the boxes slowly, their work is made easier.

How could the men do their work if they were stronger? How far would they have to move the box if they could lift it straight up? How far do they move the box when they use the plank? Which way takes longer? Which way is easier? Have they done the same amount of work each way?

Have you ever seen people lifting heavy things this way? Where? Have you ever tried it?

Tape measure

A stairway is a slope with steps on it. What would we use if we were to climb straight up? Why is it easier to use stairs?

Study the stairs in your school. Measure the height straight up. Measure the length of the stairs. How far do you move along the stairs when you raise your body one foot upwards?

Study stairs in other places. Find some stairs that are steeper than your school stairs. Are they harder to climb? How would you build stairs for old or very weak people?

Sometimes there is not enough room to build long, straight stairs. Then winding stairs are built. Such stairs may be long without taking up much space.

110

Ramp

Sometimes people must raise things that roll or have wheels. Stairs cannot be used to raise such things.

Slopes can be built without steps. Such slopes are called ramps. The picture above shows a ramp.

Why are ramps sometimes built in hospitals? Why are there ramps in many garages? Are there any ramps in your school?

To raise very heavy things, would you build a long or a short ramp? Why?

111

This boy wants to climb the hill. What is the quickest way?

If you were going to make a path for a bicycle, where would you make it?

Study a small, steep hill if you can. Measure the shortest way up the hill. Measure some other ways. Climb up the different paths and see which is easiest.

Make a path that winds back and forth. Measure it. Is it easy to climb?

A road that climbs a steep mountain often has sharp
bends in it. Can you tell why the road is made this
way?

Winding roads like this are made in most places
where there are mountains. Look for pictures of roads
made this way.

Look for pictures of railroads that are built over
mountains. Do the railroads go straight up or do they
wind up the side of the mountains?

Screws to Make Work Easier

This man is lifting one corner of a house. He is not strong enough to lift it without help. He is using a tool called a **screw jack.**

The man pushes on the bar that turns the screw. As the screw turns, it rises and pushes up the house.

Have you ever seen a screw jack being used? Where? Sometimes you will see screw jacks being used to raise heavy cars and trucks.

Try to find a screw jack that you can bring to school and show your classmates.

This drawing shows why a screw jack helps a person raise a heavy load.

The large black circle shows how far the man must move to turn the screw once. The black arrow in the center shows how far the house is raised for one turn of the screw. The man must move a long way to raise the house a short distance. He does the work very slowly.

Such tools never give us something for nothing. The man seems to be made stronger when he uses the screw jack, but he pays for it by moving farther. He does his work more slowly.

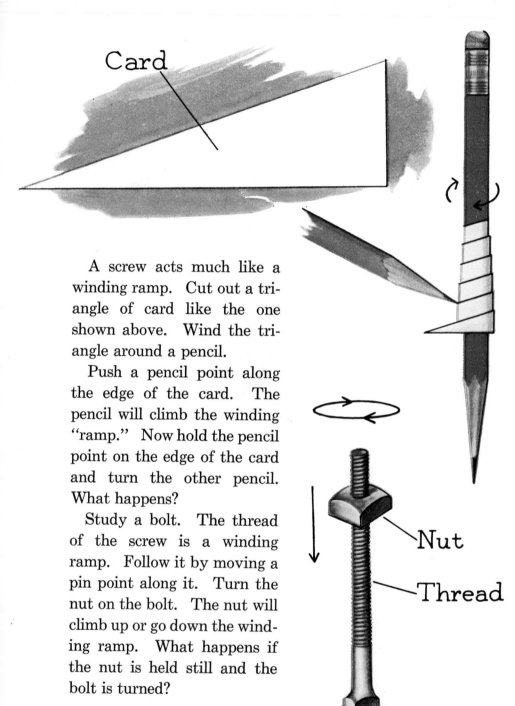

Card

A screw acts much like a winding ramp. Cut out a triangle of card like the one shown above. Wind the triangle around a pencil.

Push a pencil point along the edge of the card. The pencil will climb the winding "ramp." Now hold the pencil point on the edge of the card and turn the other pencil. What happens?

Study a bolt. The thread of the screw is a winding ramp. Follow it by moving a pin point along it. Turn the nut on the bolt. The nut will climb up or go down the winding ramp. What happens if the nut is held still and the bolt is turned?

Nut

Thread

116

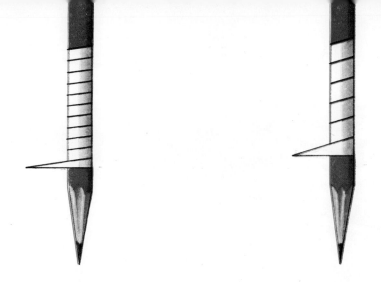

Cut out triangles of different slopes and wind each one around a pencil. What is the difference in their appearances?

A screw with threads close together has a gentle slope. It does work slowly and easily. Such screws are used to raise heavy loads.

Look for some tools that use screws. Study a meat grinder, a vise, and a wood auger. What does the screw do in each one?

Vise Screw

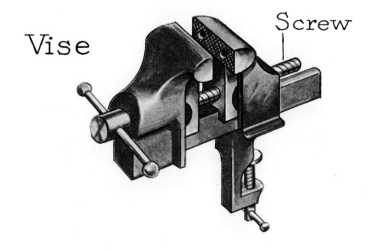

Book end

Experiments with Levers

Tie some books together with a cord. Fasten them to a stick and put a support under the stick as shown above. Push down on the stick. Then lift the books without using the stick. Which way is easier?

The stick is used as a lever. Levers are often used this way to move heavy things more easily.

Measure the distance you raise the books with the lever. Measure the distance you push down on the lever. Which is greater? Did the lever make you work through a longer distance?

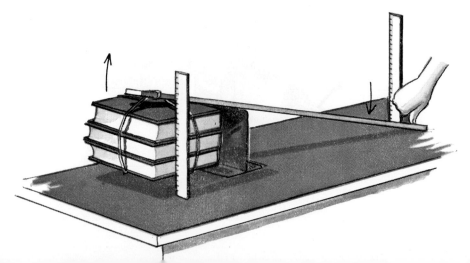

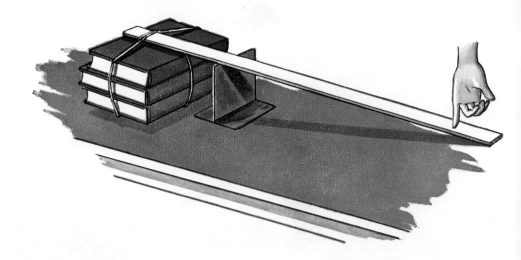

Move the support to different places. Each time raise the books by pushing down with one finger. Where is the support when the books are raised most easily?

Measure the distance the books are moved each time. Measure the distance your finger moves each time. Notice that when your finger moves farther than the books, the lever makes your work easier.

When the books move up farther than your finger moves down do you have to push harder?

119

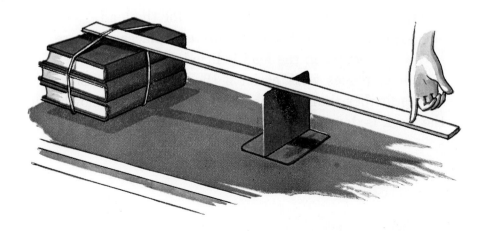

Using Levers

A lever is often used to lift heavy things. In the picture each boy is lifting a rock with a lever. Each boy is trying it a different way.

Try the experiment yourself. Use a board for a lever. Use a rock or a box of books for the load. Try the support for the lever in different places. Where is the support when the load is lifted more easily?

A lever makes work easier if the end that is pushed moves farther than the load moves. The more slowly the work is done, the easier it is to do.

A hammer is used as a lever when it is pulling a nail. The end of the handle moves much farther than the nail moves. Therefore, a small force on the handle makes a strong pull on the nail.

Try to pull a nail without a hammer. Then pull the nail with the hammer. Try to pull nails with your hand at different places on the handle of the hammer. Where is your hand when the nail comes out most easily?

Try to experiment with a wheelbarrow. If you cannot use one, use a long board with one end resting on a box.

Put a load as near the wheel as you can. How far does the load rise when you raise the handles? How far do your hands rise?

Put the load as far from the wheel as you can. How far does the load rise when you raise the handles? Does the load rise more or less than it did before?

Where is the load when it is most easily raised?

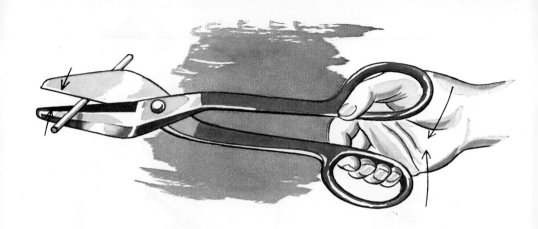

Shears like these are used to cut metal. Do the blades or the handles move farther?

Cut some wire with a pair of metal shears. Put the wire at different places between the blades. Where is the wire when it is most easily cut?

Shears are like a pair of levers working together. Name some other tools that are somewhat like shears. How is each one used? Try out as many of them as you can.

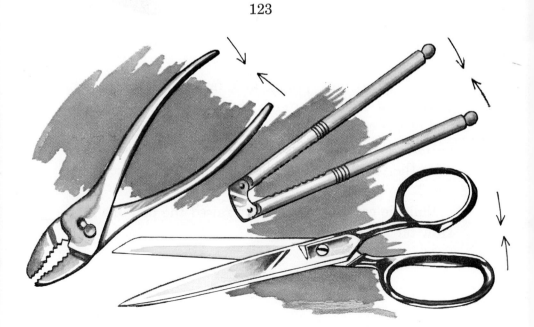

Pulleys to Help Us

Find an awning pulley and fasten it to a pail of sand. Put a cord through the pulley and fasten one end of the cord to something higher than the pail.

Raise the pail by taking hold of the handle. Then raise the pail by pulling the cord. Which is the easier way?

Pull the cord until you have raised the pail one foot. How far did your hand move?

124

Double pulleys

Find some more pulleys and use them in the ways shown below. Each time measure the distance your hand must move to raise the load one foot. Find out which ways you can use the pulleys to make work easier.

You will often see pulleys being used in some of these ways. You can always tell whether they are making the work easier by noticing whether the hands that do the pulling move farther than the load moves.

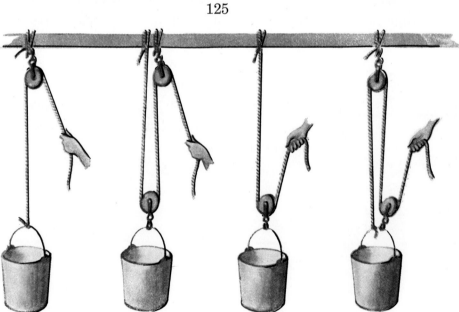

Making Friction Less

You know that it is hard to push a heavy box across the floor because the box rubs on the floor. The harder the box rubs, the harder it is to push it.

We say that there is **friction** when two parts rub together. Friction makes it hard to move the parts.

We try to make the friction as small as possible when we want to move things.

Study the pictures in this unit. Where do parts rub together and cause friction? Make a list of other places where there is friction.

126

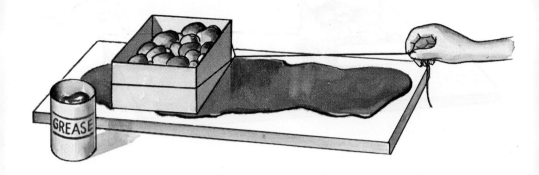

Put a load of stones in a small wooden box and pull it along a board. Notice how hard it is to pull the box. The reason there is friction between the box and the board is because the wood is rough. The rough places catch on each other. Even if we make the boards as smooth as we can, there are still rough places that catch each other.

Cover the board with grease and pull the box along the board. Notice the difference. Putting grease or oil on parts that rub together makes friction less and work easier.

Grease fills in the rough places on sliding parts and keeps the sliding parts away from each other. The picture below shows how grease between two rough parts makes the amount of friction smaller.

127

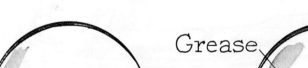

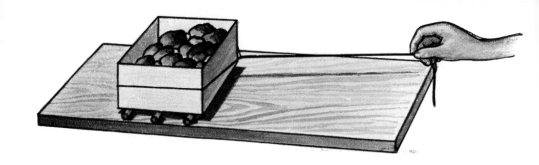

Put a load of stones in a small box and pull it along a board. Notice how hard it is to pull the box. Now put round pencils or round sticks under the box. Notice how much more easily the box moves.

Friction between rolling parts is less than friction between sliding parts. That is the reason why we use wheels on wagons and automobiles. We slide things only when there is little friction, such as when we pull a sled over ice.

The picture below shows two men moving a heavy boat into the water. What are they using? Why is this easier than sliding the boat across the beach?

128

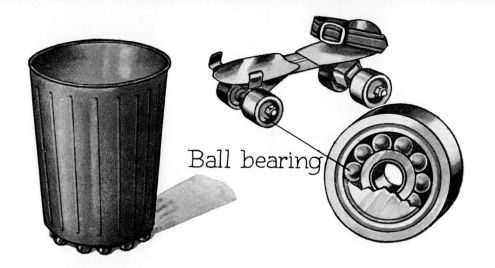

Ball bearing

Wheels rub on their axles when they turn. One way to make the friction less is to put small balls between a wheel and its axle. This is called a **ball bearing.** Sometimes small rollers are used instead of balls. This is called a **roller bearing.**

Set a wastebasket on some marbles. Turn the basket around and notice how easily it moves. There is less friction when the basket rolls on the balls than when it slides on the floor.

You will find ball bearings in many wheels. Look for them in roller skates. You can also find them in bicycle wheels and pedals.

Some automobile wheels turn on ball bearings. Other wheels turn on roller bearings. Perhaps you can see some of these bearings at a garage.

129

Roller bearing

Using Stored Energy to Make Work Easier

We use stored energy to help us with our work. We use the energy stored in gasoline and coal. List some ways we use the energy of gasoline and coal.

Running water also has energy. Explain how we use this energy.

1. Why do roads wind up mountains instead of climbing straight up?
2. How does a screw jack help us raise heavy loads?
3. What is an easy way to raise a heavy barrel into a truck?
4. Why are handles of metal shears longer than the handles of cloth shears?
5. Where is the best place to put the support of a lever when you must raise a heavy load?
6. Why are oil and grease used in automobiles?
7. What can you do to move a heavy box across a floor more easily?

Musical Sounds

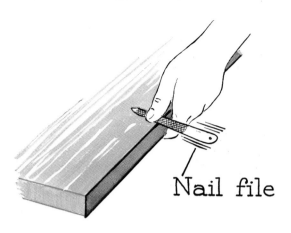

Nail file

The Cause of Sound

Hold one end of a nail file flat against a table top. Pull down the other end of the file and let it go. You will hear a sound. You will also see the file moving rapidly up and down. We say that the file **vibrates.**

Stretch a wire between two screw eyes in a board. Put a small piece of wood under the wire to tighten it. Now pluck the wire so that it moves rapidly back and forth. Look closely at it to see it vibrate. Put little folds of paper on the wire and watch them. Does the wire give off a sound when it vibrates?

Tuning fork

Sometimes you cannot see things vibrate but you can feel them. Rap a tuning fork or a table fork against a piece of wood. Touch the fork lightly to your cheek.

Hold the handle of a vibrating tuning fork against a table top. Touch the table top with your fingers. Can you feel the table vibrating?

Often you can feel a radio or a phonograph vibrating when you touch it with your fingers. When a big pipe organ is played in church, you can sometimes feel the building vibrating.

133

Tuning fork

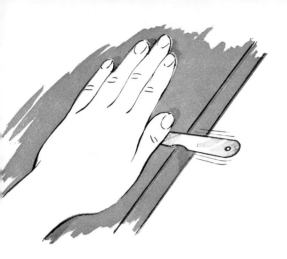

The Pitch of Sounds

Hold a nail file against a table as you held it before. Make the nail file vibrate and listen to the sound.

Hold the nail file so that a smaller part of it is able to vibrate. Make the nail file vibrate again and listen to the sound.

You will notice that the nail file vibrates more rapidly when the part that vibrates is shorter. You will also notice that the tone changes.

Try the experiment several times. Let different lengths of the file vibrate.

do re mi fa so la ti do

The sound of your voice changes as you sing a scale. You change the **pitch** of your voice.

You raise the pitch of your voice when you sing a scale like the one written above. The last note has a higher pitch than the first note.

You changed the pitch of the sound in the experiment with the nail file. The sound had a higher pitch when the nail file vibrated more rapidly.

The keys of a piano make sounds of different pitch. The keys at the right make sounds of high pitch. The keys at the left make sounds of low pitch.

135

do re mi fa so la ti do

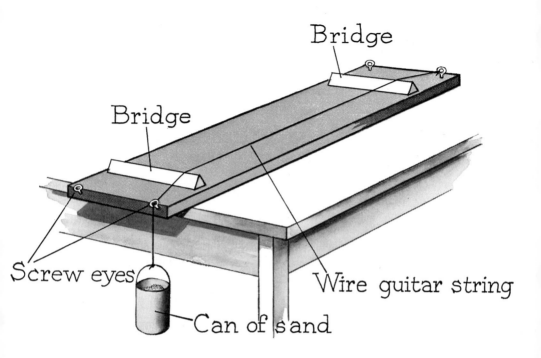

Bridge

Bridge

Screw eyes

Can of sand

Wire guitar string

Vibrating Strings

Some experiments will show you how stringed instruments like violins give off sounds of different pitch. You will need a board, some screw eyes, some guitar strings, and some cans.

Build the apparatus shown in the picture. You can whittle the bridges from small pieces of wood. Fill the can half full of sand.

Pluck the string between the bridges and listen to the sound. Move the bridges closer together and pluck the string again. What happens to the sound as the vibrating part of the string becomes shorter?

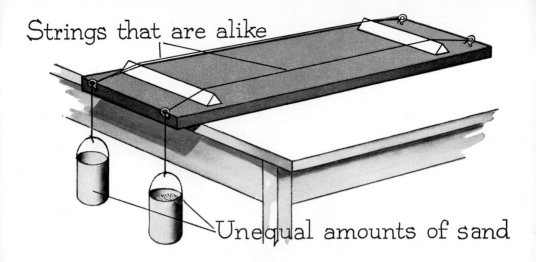

Strings that are alike

Unequal amounts of sand

Fasten two strings that are alike on the board. Put more sand in one can than in the other. Which string is tighter? Pluck each string. Which string has the higher pitch?

Add more sand to the cans. What happens to the pitch of the sound as the strings become tighter?

Fasten a thin string and a thick string to the board. Use the same amount of sand in each can so that they are equally tight. Which string has the higher pitch?

You have discovered three ways to change the pitch of vibrating strings. Write down what you have discovered.

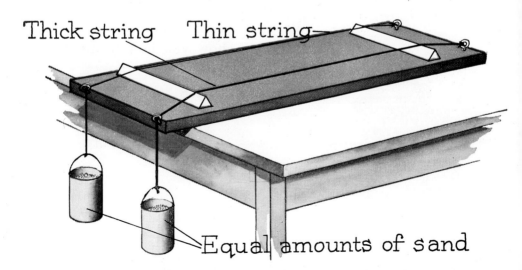

Thick string   Thin string

Equal amounts of sand

Stringed Instruments

There are three ways of changing the pitch of guitar strings. Thick strings are used for low notes. Thin ones are used for high notes. The player tunes each string by turning a key. He tightens the key to give the string a higher pitch.

When a player wants to play different notes, he presses the strings to the neck of the guitar. This makes the vibrating part of each string shorter so that it gives off higher notes.

Watch someone playing a guitar. Ask him to show you how he tunes the strings.

138

Most of the instruments in big orchestras are members of the violin family. Four instruments of the violin family are shown below.

Look at the picture of the man playing the violin. Notice how he changes the pitch of a string by making the vibrating part shorter. How does he make the string vibrate?

Which of the four instruments shown below should give off the lowest notes? How are the strings tuned?

Bass viol

Violin   Viola

Violoncello

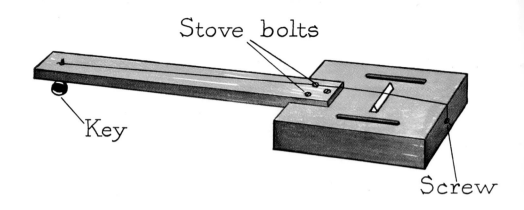

Stove bolts

Key

Screw

Homemade Stringed Instruments

You can make a guitar from a cigar box. Use a jackknife to cut two slots in the bottom of the cigar box. Saw out a board for the neck of the guitar and fasten it to the box with three stove bolts. Then nail the cover shut.

Whittle a key or buy a violin key at a music store. Bore a hole in the neck for the key. The key must fit tightly in the hole. Then whittle a bridge or buy one.

Fasten one end of a wire guitar string to a screw in the end of the cigar box. Wind the other end on the key. Tighten the string and you can play a tune on the guitar.

140

Neck

Bridge

Stove bolt

You can also make a violin with a broomstick and a board. You will need a violin bow to play it.

Fasten the board to the broomstick with short screws. Mark the place where the key should go with a small nail hole. This nail hole will make it easier to start boring the hole for the key. Finish your violin as shown in the picture.

You can play real tunes on this violin. You can make marks on the board so that you will know where to put your fingers for the different notes.

141

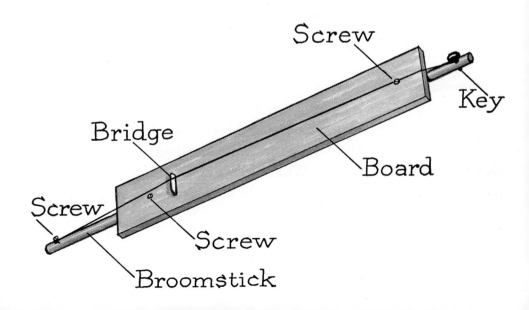

Screw

Key

Board

Bridge

Screw

Screw

Broomstick

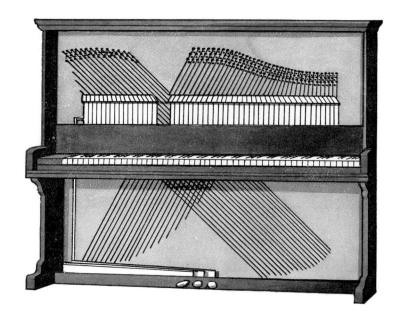

The Piano

Ask someone to take off the front of an upright piano so that you can study it. Look at the strings. Which strings are longest? Which are thickest? Which strings have the highest pitch? Notice the way the strings are fastened. Can you see how the piano tuner changes the pitch of the strings?

Press a piano key slowly. Notice what happens. What does the hammer do?

Find the dampers. The dampers rest on the strings and keep them from vibrating. Watch a damper when you play a note. What happens? Press on the damper pedal and play some notes. What happens?

142

Hammers

Dampers

The Harp

A harp is somewhat like a piano. There are many strings. Some strings are longer and thicker than other strings. Some strings are tighter than others.

The harp is played by plucking the strings. How are the strings of a piano made to vibrate?

You can make a simple harp by nailing three boards together in the shape of a triangle. Fasten one end

Harp

of each string to a screw on one side of the triangle. Fasten the other end of each string to a screw eye. Tune the strings by turning the screw eyes. Tune the strings to match the notes of a piano. Then you can play tunes on the harp.

143

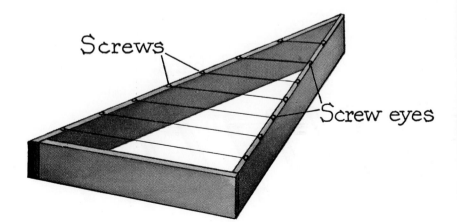

Screws

Screw eyes

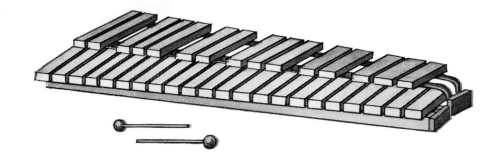

The Xylophone

The musical notes of a xylophone come from bars of wood. The bars are struck with little hammers to make them vibrate. There are other musical instruments that have bars of metal that vibrate.

You can make a xylophone from pieces of broom handles. Cut eight pieces to the following lengths:

10 inches	$9\frac{7}{16}$ inches	$8\frac{15}{16}$ inches
$8\frac{11}{16}$ inches	$8\frac{3}{16}$ inches	$7\frac{12}{16}$ inches
$7\frac{5}{16}$ inches	$7\frac{1}{16}$ inches	

Tie the bars together with two stout strings as shown below. Play them by hitting them with a golf ball on a small stick. You may need to tune the bars. Whittle off the end of a bar to raise the pitch. Whittle a little wood from the middle to lower the pitch.

144

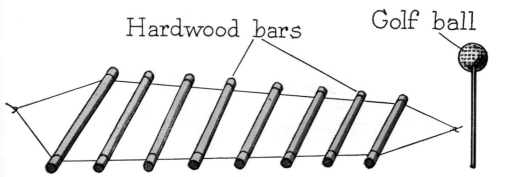

Hardwood bars   Golf ball

A set of musical glasses is something like a xylophone. Find some drinking glasses that ring when you tap them with a pencil. Pour a little water into one of the glasses. Does the water raise or lower the pitch of the glass?

Pick up eight glasses and tune them to the notes of the scale by putting water in them. Tap them with a pencil. You can play simple tunes on them.

You may also use bottles instead of drinking glasses. Tune them with water just as you tuned the glasses.

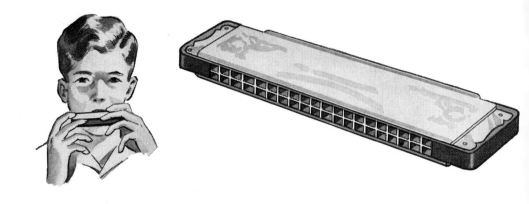

Reeds

Perhaps you can take a mouth organ apart to see what is inside. Notice the little strips of metal that make the sounds. These strips are called **reeds.**

A reed vibrates when air blows past it. Short reeds give sounds of high pitch. Long reeds give sounds of low pitch.

Reeds are used in accordions. Each key on the accordion opens a valve that lets air blow past a reed. The air comes from the bellows of the accordion. Watch someone play an accordion and notice what he does.

146

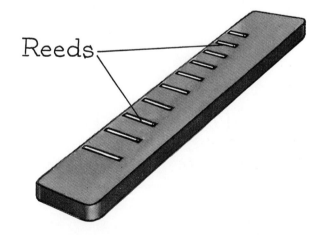

Reeds

Vibrating Columns of Air

Blow over the top of a bottle to make a musical sound. Now put a little water in the bottle and blow across its top again. Did the water raise or lower the pitch of the sound?

Scientists tell us that the column of air in the bottle vibrates when you blow across the top of the bottle. The vibrating air gives out the sound. When you put water in the bottle you made the air column shorter and raised its pitch.

Bring eight bottles to school. Tune the bottles by putting water in them so that you can play a musical scale on them.

147

Water

Whistles

Whistles make sounds in the same way that bottles make sounds when you blow over them. There is an opening in a tube. Air is blown past this opening. This makes the column of air in the whistle vibrate.

Bring different kinds of whistles to school. Find the column of air in each one. Find the opening that you blow past.

You can make a whistle from a piece of hollow wood such as bamboo. Cut a notch in the side of the tube as shown in the picture. Whittle a plug that almost closes the tube. When you blow the whistle, air goes out the notch. As it goes out, it makes the column of air in the tube vibrate.

148

Plug

Air

Air column

Plug

A long whistle has a long column of air. It gives off a low note. A short whistle has a short column of air. It gives off a high note.

You can change the length of the air column in a slide whistle. Pull the slide out to make a low note and push it in to make a high note. You can play tunes on the whistle.

Another whistle has holes along the side. You can cover the holes with your fingers. With all holes covered, the column of air is as long as the whistle. When you uncover a hole, the vibrating column of air becomes shorter.

Bring some whistles like these to school and study them.

149

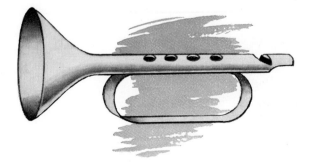

Wind Instruments

A flute is somewhat like a whistle. The player blows over a hole in the flute just as you blow over a bottle. He changes the pitch of the flute by opening or closing holes in the flute. The pitch of the sound is low when all the holes are covered, because the air column is as long as the flute.

A clarinet has a reed in the mouthpiece. The reed vibrates and makes the column of air in the clarinet vibrate. The player changes the pitch much as a flute player does.

150

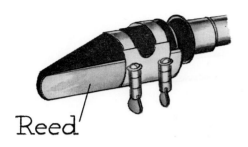

Reed

A saxophone is a good instrument for study. Perhaps someone can bring one to school for you to look at.

Notice the reed. The reed vibrates when the player blows on the saxophone. The reed makes the air column in the saxophone vibrate.

Notice the holes in the saxophone. The holes are covered by pressing on keys. Ask someone to play the saxophone and notice how he changes the pitch.

Visit a music store and look at the different sizes of saxophones. Do you think the large saxophones or the small saxophones have the lower pitch?

Trombone

A trombone is another kind of wind instrument. The player makes the air in the trombone vibrate by vibrating his lips. Ask someone to show you how he holds his lips to do this.

A trombone has a long air column which makes low notes. The player can change the pitch by sliding part of the trombone in or out. This makes the air column shorter or longer.

The pictures on this page show how the player changes the pitch. The top picture shows the slide pushed out. The air column is long and a low note is being played. The bottom picture shows the slide pulled in. The air column is short and a higher note is being played.

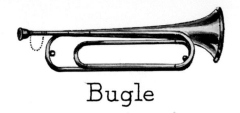

Bugle

Imagine that you could straighten out a bugle. It would look like the one in the picture at the left. The air column would be as long in the straight bugle as in the coiled bugle. What is the advantage of the coiled bugle?

Look at the pictures of other kinds of horns. Imagine that each one could be straightened out. Guess how long each one would be.

Use a string to measure the air column in a horn. Hold one end of the string at the mouthpiece. Lay the string along the horn so that it follows every curve. Cut off the string at the large end of the horn. Now straighten out the string and see how long it is.

153

French horn

Tuba

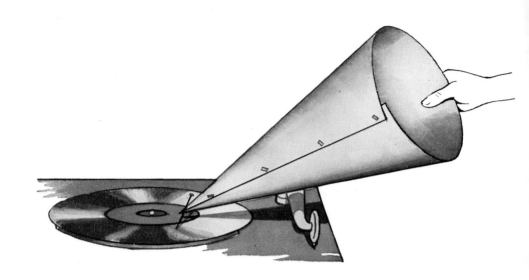

Storing Sounds

This experiment will help you understand how sounds are stored on a phonograph record.

Make a horn of light cardboard. Push a needle or a pin through the small end of the horn. Rest the needle on a phonograph record that is turning around. What happens?

Look at a phonograph record with a hand lens. Notice the grooves. The waves in the grooves make the needle vibrate. This causes the sound.

In the picture find the groove that makes the needle vibrate most rapidly.

154

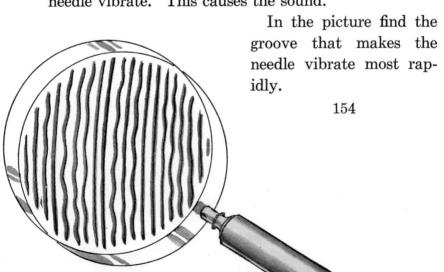

You can see record-making machines in radio stations. Some people also have them to make records for their own use.

A record-making machine has a needle that cuts a groove in a record. The needle vibrates rapidly when there is a high-pitched sound. Then the groove has many waves close together. The needle vibrates more slowly for low-pitched sounds. Then the waves are farther apart. The groove is straight when there is no sound.

The records you buy are molded from master records made in this way. Several thousand records may be molded from one master record.

There are other kinds of machines used for storing sounds. Some store sounds in wire and others in tape. You must know more about electricity and magnetism to understand how they work. You can see these machines in radio stations, in some homes, and in business offices. Find out how they are used.

Tape recorder

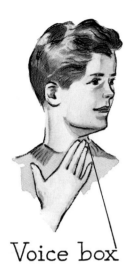

Voice box

The Voice Box

Press your fingers to your throat and find a tube that seems to be made up of hard rings. This is your windpipe.

Find the hard bump that seems to move when you swallow. This is your voice box. It is at the top of the windpipe.

There are two cords stretched across the voice box. They vibrate when you blow air past them. Put your fingers on your voice box as you hum. Notice the vibrations.

You tighten the cords to make sounds of high pitch. You loosen the cords to make sounds of low pitch.

Make a model voice box with a funnel and two pieces of rubber from a balloon. Tie the pieces on the funnel so that there is a narrow slit between them. Blow through the funnel.

156

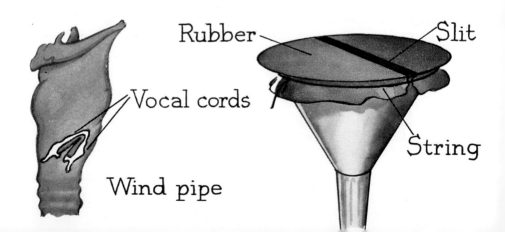

Rubber   Slit

Vocal cords

String

Wind pipe

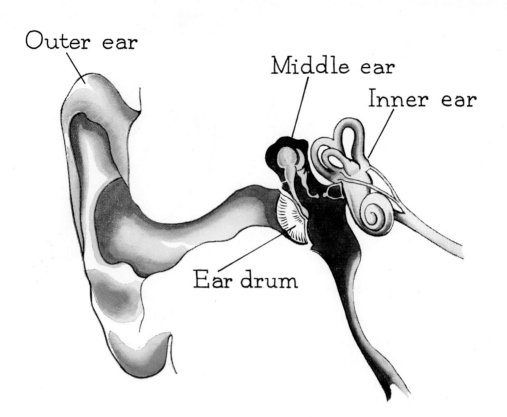

Outer ear

Middle ear

Inner ear

Ear drum

Our Ears

Most of the sounds you hear come through the air. These sounds are brought to you by vibrating air.

Vibrating air makes your ear drums vibrate. This makes some tiny bones in your middle ears vibrate. The bones in their turn make your inner ears vibrate.

Nerves in the inner ears send messages to your brain telling whether your ears are vibrating rapidly or slowly. From the messages, you know whether you are listening to a high-pitched sound or a low-pitched sound.

157

Bird Voices

Birds have voice boxes somewhat like ours. Many of them also have a second voice box at the bottom of the windpipe.

Such birds use the second voice box for most of their singing. Birds make some of their call notes and alarm notes with the upper voice box.

---

1. What causes sound?
2. How can you change the pitch of a vibrating string?
3. Which bars of a xylophone have the highest pitch?
4. How do you make sounds when you speak or sing?
5. If you add water to a bottle what happens to the pitch of the sound you make when you blow over it?
6. How do most sounds come to your ears?
7. How is the pitch of a flute changed?

Some Common Acids

Vinegar and Baking Soda

Fill a glass nearly full of water and dissolve a teaspoonful of baking soda in it. Add a little vinegar and stir it. What do you see in the liquid?

Put a teaspoonful of baking soda in a glass. Pour in some vinegar. What happens? Try the experiment again. Does the same thing happen?

Light a match and hold it in the glass. What happens to the flame? Try this several times. Does the same thing happen each time?

160

The bubbles that you see in the mixture of vinegar and baking soda are bubbles of a gas called carbon dioxide.

Put some vinegar and baking soda in a bottle. Hold your thumb over the mouth of the bottle. Notice how the gas pushes your thumb. It may even push your thumb away from the mouth of the bottle.

Take the bottle outdoors. Put the bottle in a can. Pour in a few tablespoonfuls of vinegar and the same amount of water. Then put in a teaspoonful of baking soda. Put a cork in the bottle and stand back. What happens?

161

Acids in Foods

There are many liquids that give off bubbles of carbon dioxide when baking soda is mixed with them. Try lemon juice, orange juice, grapefruit juice, and tomato juice. Try some other foods when you go home.

Taste the different foods that bubble when they are mixed with baking soda. Most of the foods will taste sour.

Things that are sour and that give off bubbles when mixed with baking soda are called **acids.** There are acids in many of our foods. Do you know of any other acids?

Dry Acids

Your mother may use a chemical called cream of tartar when she bakes. Taste a bit of this chemical. How does it taste?

Mix a teaspoonful of cream of tartar with a teaspoonful of baking soda. What happens? Add half a cup of water. What happens?

This experiment shows that water must be added before cream of tartar and baking soda will give off carbon dioxide. Water is often needed when chemicals are used together.

There are other dry acids besides cream of tartar. Boric acid is a common dry acid.

163

Baking Powder

Most cooks use baking powder. Look in a cookbook for some foods that have baking powder in them.

The label on the can tells what is in baking powder. Collect the labels from cans of different kinds of baking powder.

There is baking soda in all baking powders. Sometimes the baking soda is called bicarbonate of soda. There is also a dry acid in all baking powders. Sometimes the acid is cream of tartar.

Put a teaspoonful of baking powder in a glass of water. What happens?

164

For this next experiment it is best to use a baking powder that is made with cream of tartar.

Mix a teaspoonful of the baking powder with half a glass of flour. Add just enough water to moisten the flour. Mix the flour and water rapidly. Then watch the mixture through the glass.

Baking powder makes bubbles of carbon dioxide in the dough. The bubbles make the dough rise. Look at cake and biscuits for holes left by bubbles of gas.

Make some biscuits with baking powder. At the same time make some biscuits without baking powder. How are they different?

165

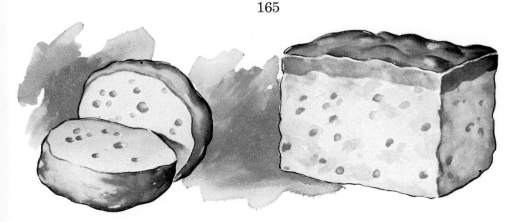

RECIPE MOLASSES CAKE
½ cup shortening   3 eggs
½ cup sugar   ¾ teaspoon baking soda
⅔ cup molasses   ½ cup milk
2¼ cups flour   1 teaspoon salt
½ cup raisins   1 teaspoon cinnamon

Baking Without Baking Powder

This cake has no baking powder in it, but it rises like other cakes. The recipe shows that there is baking soda in the cake. There must also be an acid in the recipe.

Test each of the things in the recipe to find the acid. Test them with baking soda just as you tested lemon juice and cream of tartar. You should find some acid in the molasses.

Look at recipes for cakes, cookies, and biscuits. Find recipes that call for baking soda. Then test the things in these recipes to find out whether any of them contain acids.

RECIPE   SOFT GINGERBREAD

1 cup molasses   1 teaspoon baking soda
3 tablespoons shortening ⅔ cup sugar
2 teaspoons ginger   1 teaspoon salt
2 cups flour   1 cup water

This is another cake that does not use baking powder. Does the name of the cake tell you where the acid is?

Try to get some sour milk or sour cream. Test it with baking soda. Is there an acid in it? Buttermilk is left after the butter is taken from sour cream. Test some buttermilk to see if there is an acid in it.

When cooks do not have sour cream, they sometimes use fresh cream. Then they add a little vinegar or lemon juice in the recipe for sour cream cake. Tell why the cake rises.

167

Acids and Milk

Put a drop of vinegar or lemon juice in a spoonful of milk. What happens? Perhaps you have seen the same thing happen when you put cream on strawberries. Acids make milk curdle.

Cream of tomato soup is made with tomatoes and milk. The acid in the tomatoes curdles the milk. Some people do not like to see curdled milk in soup, so cooks often put a little baking soda in the tomatoes before the milk is added. The acid unites with the soda instead of curdling the milk.

168

Curds

Whey

Sour skim milk

Sour milk cheese

You have seen that there is an acid in sour milk. This acid curdles the milk. That is why sour milk is always curdled.

Thick, white curds rise to the top of sour milk after it has been standing for a while. The curds may be skimmed off and made into cheese. For thousands of years, cheese has been made from the curds of sour milk.

The acid in sour milk comes from certain bacteria that live in milk. These bacteria are not harmful, but there may be other bacteria that are harmful living with them. Milk is pasteurized to kill these harmful bacteria. Pasteurized milk is safe to drink.

169

Sour milk bacteria

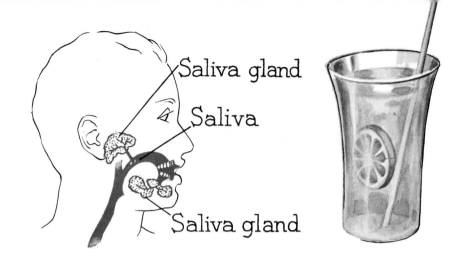

Acids and Digestion

At your next meal eat a bit of pickle before you eat anything else. Notice how fast the saliva comes from your saliva glands. Perhaps it is flowing rapidly right now as you think about pickles.

Foods with acids in them often make saliva flow faster, and the foods become easier to swallow. Vinegar is used in pickles and salad dressing. It is put on such foods as beans and greens. Lemon juice is put on fish. Some people like to start a meal with a small glass of tomato juice.

170

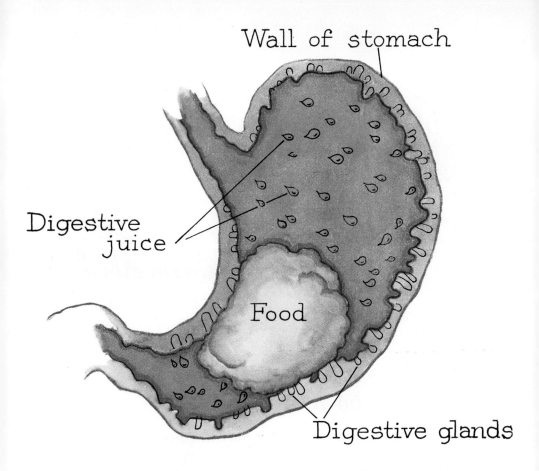

Wall of stomach

Digestive
   juice

Food

Digestive glands

There are many glands in the walls of the stomach. These glands give off a digestive juice. There is an acid in the digestive juice.

This acid is important. It starts the muscles of the stomach working. It helps other chemicals in the digestive juice dissolve certain kinds of food. It starts other glands working to give out digestive juices.

The acid in the stomach also kills many bacteria in our food. This keeps the food from spoiling when it is in our stomachs. Unluckily for us, there are some disease bacteria that this acid cannot kill.

Teeth injured by
sucking lemons

Harmful Acids

Strong acids in food may dissolve some
of the enamel from our teeth. We cannot
grow new enamel, so we should be careful
about eating too many of these foods.

It is not wise to suck lemons. Lemon
juice can dissolve the enamel. Many
people have harmed their teeth by doing
this. Mix the lemon juice with water
before drinking it.

There are some drinks that are made
with phosphoric acid. Scientists have
learned that this acid can dissolve the
enamel from teeth.

Some dangerous acids

The acids we have been studying are rather weak acids. They are harmless or nearly so. There are other acids that are dangerous. They can burn your skin and harm your eyes. They are deadly poison if you drink them. They can make holes in cloth and dissolve metals.

A dangerous acid is used in the storage battery of an automobile. This acid is sulphuric acid.

Always be careful with acids. Never experiment with them unless you know that they are safe.

173

Storage battery

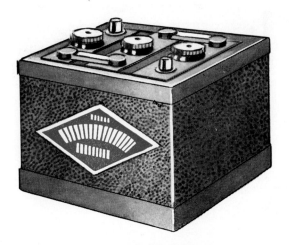

The Soda-Acid Fire Extinguisher

The soda-acid fire extinguisher must be turned up-side down before it is used.

There is water with baking soda dissolved in it. There is also a bottle of sulphuric acid inside the extinguisher.

When the extinguisher is turned over, the acid runs from the bottle and mixes with the baking soda in the water. Carbon dioxide gas is given off. As soon as the extinguisher is turned over, the pressure of the gas in the extinguisher forces the water out the hose with great force.

174

Carbon dioxide

Baking soda in water

Acid

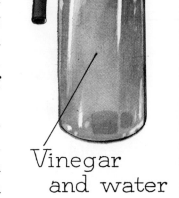

Baking soda
in paper

Make a model fire extinguisher with a
bottle. Put a short piece of glass tubing
in a cork that has one hole in it. Slip a
piece of rubber tubing on the glass tube.
The rubber tubing will be the hose of
the extinguisher.

Pour a mixture made with half vinegar and half water into the bottle.
Roll a teaspoonful of baking soda in a
bit of tissue paper and hang it by a
thread above the liquid in the bottle.

Vinegar
and water

Go outdoors and turn the bottle upside down. Point
the tube at a piece of burning paper.

175

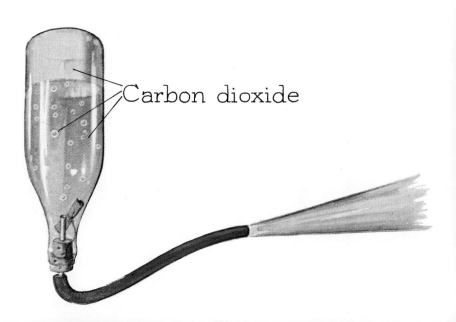

Carbon dioxide

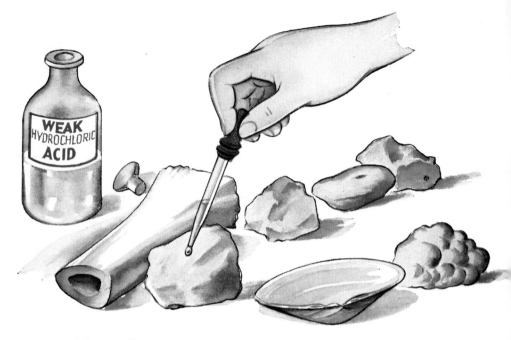

Acid and Rocks

Weak hydrochloric acid can be used to test rocks for limestone. If the rock makes the acid bubble, it is usually limestone.

Put drops of weak hydrochloric acid on different rocks. Which ones are limestone?

Put drops of the acid on shells and bones. Do they bubble too? Limestone is usually made up of bits of shells. You can often see the remains of the shells in limestone.

Test a piece of concrete. The cement in the concrete is made from limestone.

Limestone

Put a small piece of limestone or concrete in a small jar of weak acid. What happens to the limestone? What happens to the concrete?

There are often weak acids in streams. What do you think happens when such a stream flows over limestone for many years?

Rain also has a little weak acid in it. Look at some marble monuments that have been standing for many years. Do you see any signs that make you think the acid has been changing the marble?

Plants give off weak acids from their roots. The acids help break down pieces of limestone in the soil. Thus the plants help change rocks into soil.

177

Acids in Soil

Acid soil is common in deep woods. The plants give off acids as they grow. The decaying plants also give off acids.

Many plants grow best in acid soil. In deep woods you will find ferns, mosses, and some flowering plants that need acid soil. What plants live in the woods near your home?

178

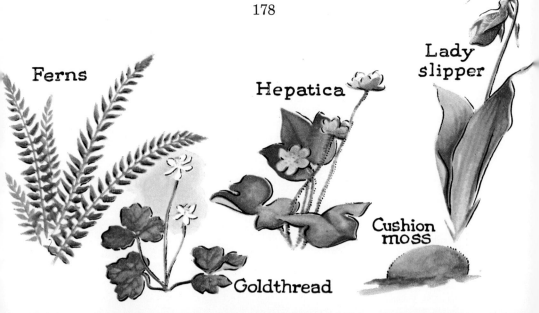

Ferns

Hepatica

Lady slipper

Cushion moss

Goldthread

Very wet places with acid soils are called bogs. Cranberries and blueberries are common in bogs. There is peat moss in most bogs. Sometimes you will also find the interesting plants that catch insects.

Cotton grass

Blueberries

Cranberries

Pitcher plant

Pogonia

Peat moss

Crops such as cabbage and clover do not grow well in an acid soil. Chemicals must be added to the soil to remove the acids. Farmers usually use lime or ground limestone to remove the acids from their fields.

---

1. Name some foods that have acid in them.
2. What gas is given off when baking soda is mixed with an acid?
3. Why is baking powder put in biscuit dough?
4. What do weak acids do to limestone?
5. Why does milk sometimes taste sour?
6. Why is a soda-acid fire extinguisher turned upside down before it is used?

Electromagnets

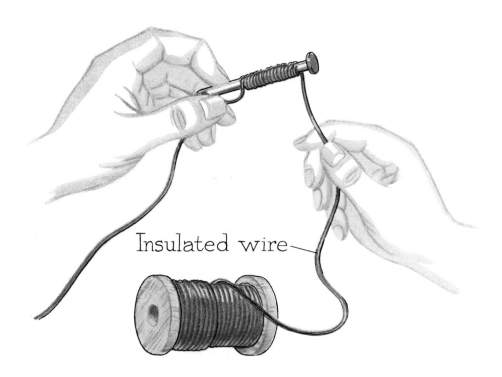

Insulated wire

Making an Electromagnet

A coil of wire becomes an electromagnet when electricity flows through the wire. The electromagnet is stronger if the wire is wound on something made of iron.

Make an electromagnet by winding insulated wire on a large nail. Twenty turns of wire will make a good magnet.

Insulated wire is wire with a covering on it. The covering may be cotton, or rubber, or anything that does not carry electricity well. Why should you use insulated wire on your electromagnet?

Wire

Insulation

It is well to use a switch when you connect the electromagnet to a dry cell. A dry cell lasts longer if electricity flows only when you need it. The best kind of switch is one that stops the electricity as soon as you take away your hand.

Hold the electromagnet near a pile of small nails. Press the switch. The electromagnet will pick up some of the nails. What happens when you stop the electric current?

Turn the electromagnet around. Can you pick up nails with the other end of it?

Try to pick up pieces of copper, wood, rubber, and other things not made of iron. Will the electromagnet pick them up?

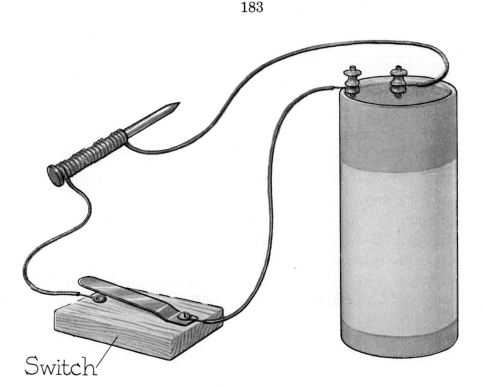

Switch

PICKED UP BY
20 TURNS

PICKED UP BY
40 TURNS

Experiments with an Electromagnet

Wind twenty turns of insulated wire on a large nail. Connect the wire to a dry cell and a switch. Find out how many small nails the electromagnet can pick up.

Wind forty turns of the same kind of wire on the nail. How many small nails will the electromagnet pick up now?

Some of you may want to try sixty turns of wire on the nail. How many nails can the electromagnet pick up with this number of turns?

When you add more turns of wire to an electromagnet, is the electromagnet stronger than it was, is it the same, or is it weaker?

Connect your electromagnet to one dry cell. Find out how many small nails the electromagnet can pick up.

Connect the electromagnet to two dry cells as shown in the picture. Two dry cells force more electricity through the wire. How many small nails can it pick up now?

Is the electromagnet stronger or weaker when more electricity flows through it?

Write down what you have discovered about your electromagnet.

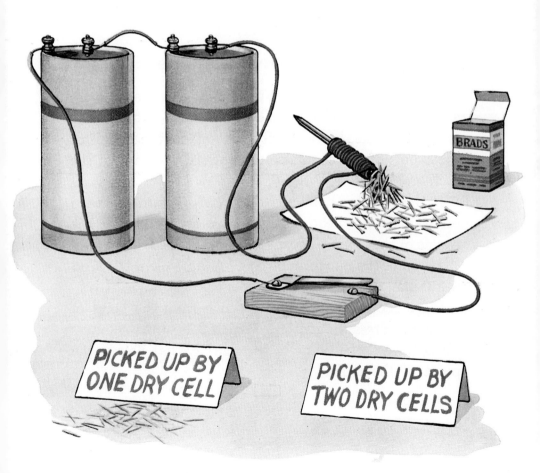

PICKED UP BY ONE DRY CELL

PICKED UP BY TWO DRY CELLS

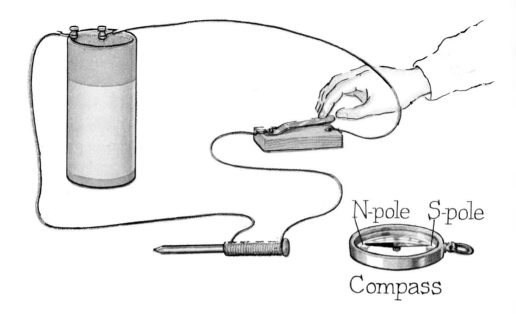

N-pole S-pole

Compass

The Poles of an Electromagnet

Lay an electromagnet on the table. Place a compass about an inch from the head of the nail. Press on the switch to make the electricity flow. Does the N-pole or the S-pole of the compass turn toward the head of the nail?

If the N-pole of the compass turns toward the head of the nail, the head of the nail is an S-pole. If the S-pole of the compass turns toward the head of the nail, the head of the nail is an N-pole. What pole is the head of the nail of your electromagnet?

Place the compass about an inch from the point of the nail. Press the switch. Which pole of the compass turns toward the point of the nail? What pole is the point of the nail?

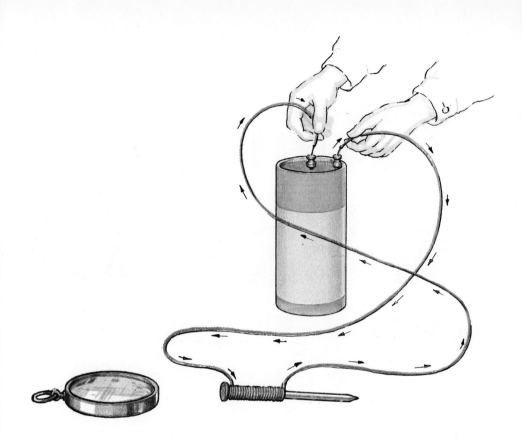

This experiment shows what happens when you change the direction in which the electricity flows.

Place a compass about an inch from one end of an electromagnet. Touch the wires to the binding posts of a dry cell. Notice which way the compass points. Mark the poles of the electromagnet.

Now change the wires so that each touches the other binding post. This makes the electricity flow in the other direction. Notice the compass. Which way is it pointing? What has happened to the poles of the electromagnet?

Electromagnet

Boom   Mast

Dry cell

Making an Electromagnetic Crane

The next few pages tell you how to make a model electromagnetic crane. This crane picks up small things made of iron, moves them to a new place, and drops them. It is like the big electromagnetic cranes that are used to load and unload steel.

You will need a board for the bottom of the crane, a block of wood, and some long, thin pieces of wood. You will need a dry cell and some insulated wire. Most of the other parts are easy to find.

Nail the block in the center of the board. Use one of the long, thin pieces of wood for the mast. Nail it to the end of the block and drive another nail up through the bottom board into the mast.

Cut two pieces of metal from a tin can and shape them like the ones in the picture. Punch three holes in each one. Fasten each to the mast with two screws.

The second long piece of wood will be the boom. Fasten it to the pieces of metal with screws. The pieces of metal act as a hinge for the boom. You may use a real hinge here if you wish.

189

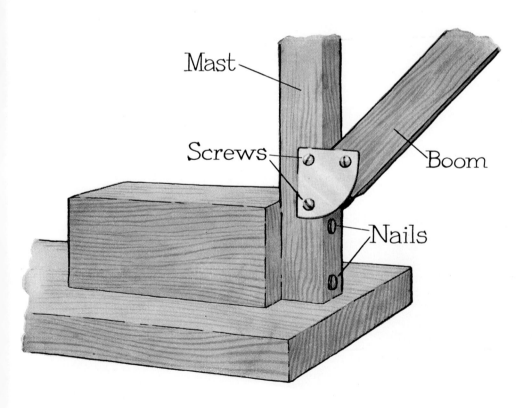

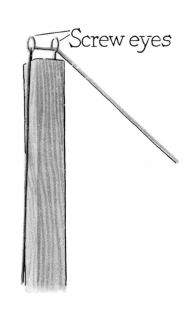
Screw eyes

The picture below shows the right hand side of the crane. Notice the lever. It is made of wood and is screwed to the block. It raises and lowers the boom.

A string goes through screw eyes from the lever over the top of the mast to the boom. Study the pictures carefully to find out where to put the screw eyes.

The dry cell is held in place by a strip of metal cut from a tin can.

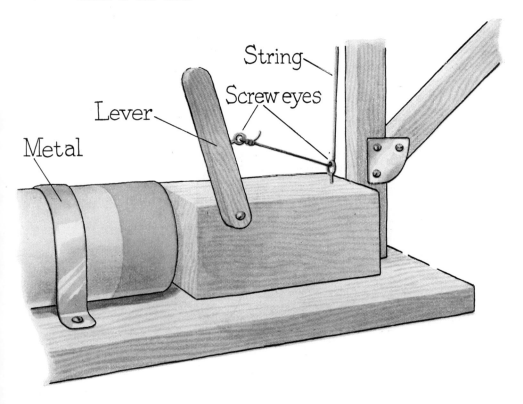

String

Screw eyes

Lever

Metal

Wire

Washers

Bolt

Put two washers on a stove bolt. Wind many turns of wire between the washers. This will be used as the electromagnet. Wrap a short piece of wire under the nut of the stove bolt and twist the wire into a loop. Fasten a string from the loop to a screw eye in the end of the boom.

One wire of the electromagnet goes to the dry cell. The other wire goes to the switch. A short wire goes from the switch to the dry cell.

Push the lever forward to lower the electromagnet into a pile of nails. Then press the switch and pull back on the lever. The magnet will lift some of the nails. Open the switch to drop the nails.

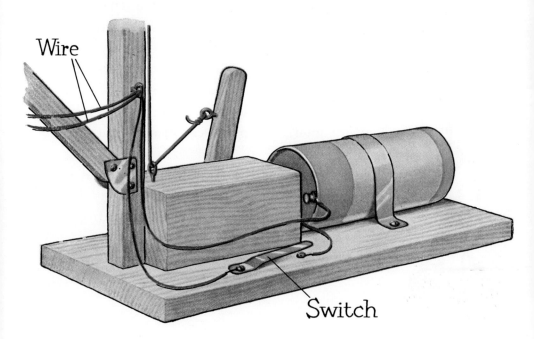

Wire

Switch

Electromagnetic Cranes in Use

Electromagnetic cranes are used to load and unload steel scrap. You can see them in junk yards and on docks where steel scrap is handled.

The man who runs the crane lowers the electromagnet into a pile of steel scrap. Then he turns on the electricity and raises the electromagnet. Many pieces of steel cling to the magnet.

Next, he moves the crane until the steel is over a railroad car, a truck, or a barge. He shuts off the electricity and the scrap drops.

192

Electromagnet

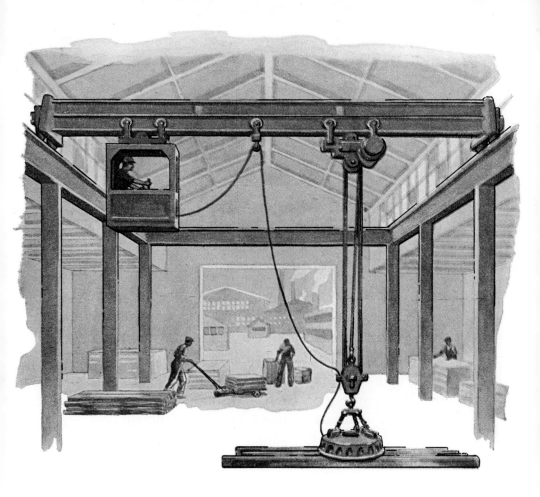

Several kinds of cranes are used for handling steel. In factories, the cranes often run on tracks near the tops of the buildings.

Electromagnets are used in factories to carry large bars and sheets of steel from one place to another. They are also used to gather up bits of scrap steel that are left around the machines.

Can electromagnetic cranes be used to handle lumber, copper, or aluminum? Explain your answer.

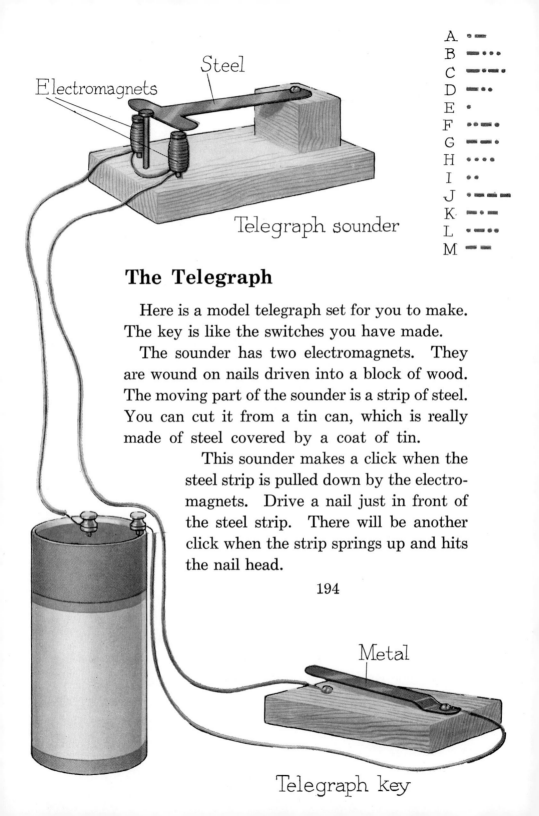

Steel

Electromagnets

Telegraph sounder

A ·—
B —···
C —·—·
D —··
E ·
F ··—·
G ——·
H ····
I ··
J ·———
K —·—
L ·—··
M ——

The Telegraph

Here is a model telegraph set for you to make. The key is like the switches you have made.

The sounder has two electromagnets. They are wound on nails driven into a block of wood. The moving part of the sounder is a strip of steel. You can cut it from a tin can, which is really made of steel covered by a coat of tin.

This sounder makes a click when the steel strip is pulled down by the electromagnets. Drive a nail just in front of the steel strip. There will be another click when the strip springs up and hits the nail head.

194

Metal

Telegraph key

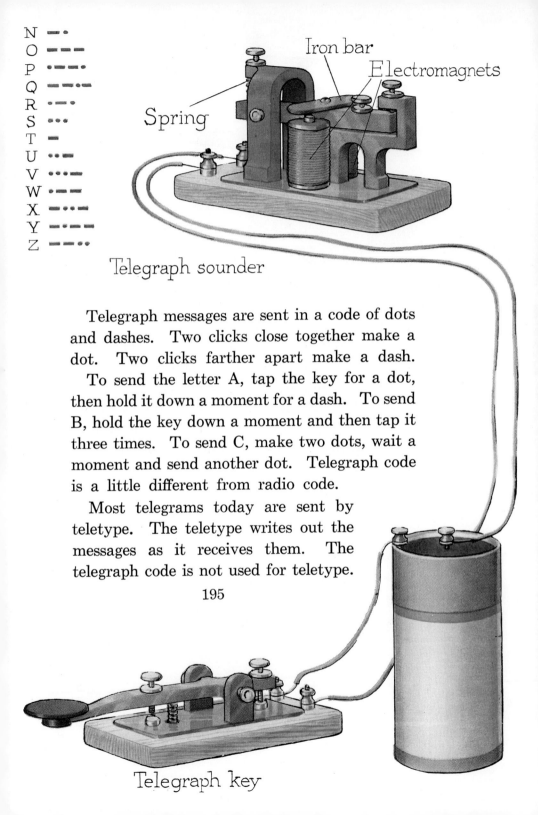

N —·
O ———
P ·——·
Q ——·—
R ·—·
S ···
T —
U ··—
V ···—
W ·——
X ——··—
Y ——·——
Z ———··

Iron bar

Electromagnets

Spring

Telegraph sounder

Telegraph messages are sent in a code of dots and dashes. Two clicks close together make a dot. Two clicks farther apart make a dash.

To send the letter A, tap the key for a dot, then hold it down a moment for a dash. To send B, hold the key down a moment and then tap it three times. To send C, make two dots, wait a moment and send another dot. Telegraph code is a little different from radio code.

Most telegrams today are sent by teletype. The teletype writes out the messages as it receives them. The telegraph code is not used for teletype.

195

Telegraph key

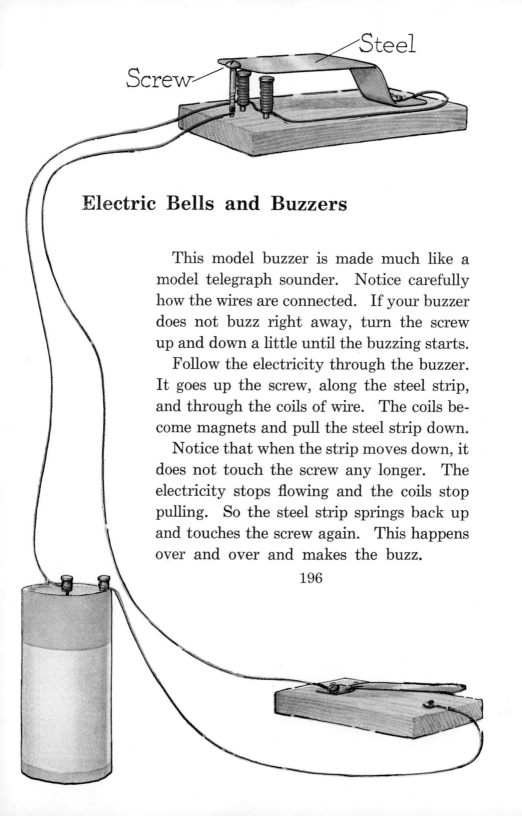

Steel

Screw

Electric Bells and Buzzers

This model buzzer is made much like a model telegraph sounder. Notice carefully how the wires are connected. If your buzzer does not buzz right away, turn the screw up and down a little until the buzzing starts.

Follow the electricity through the buzzer. It goes up the screw, along the steel strip, and through the coils of wire. The coils become magnets and pull the steel strip down.

Notice that when the strip moves down, it does not touch the screw any longer. The electricity stops flowing and the coils stop pulling. So the steel strip springs back up and touches the screw again. This happens over and over and makes the buzz.

196

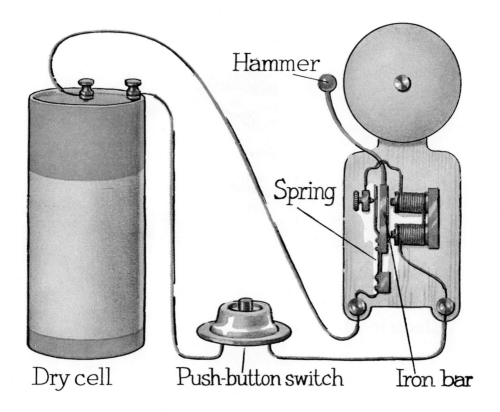

Hammer

Spring

Dry cell   Push-button switch   Iron bar

Electric bells and buzzers are made much alike. Connect an electric bell, a push button, and a dry cell. Push the button and watch the hammer move back and forth against the bell.

Find the electromagnets. Look for the iron bar near one end of the electromagnets. The hammer is fastened to this bar. Push the bar toward the coils and notice that the hammer hits the bell. Look for the spring that pulls the iron bar back when you take your finger away.

Electric bells work like the model buzzer you just made. Study the bell and see if you can explain it.

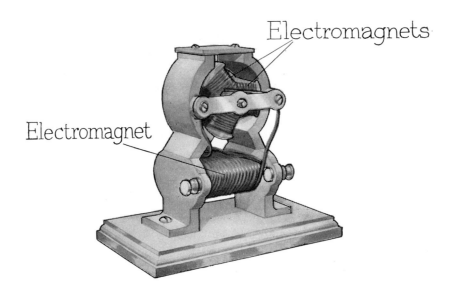

Electromagnets

Electromagnet

Electric Motors

There are electromagnets in electric motors. Look inside an electric motor. Notice the coils of wire. These are the electromagnets.

Perhaps someone will bring a toy electric motor to school. Look for the electromagnets. Connect the motor to some dry cells and watch it run.

198

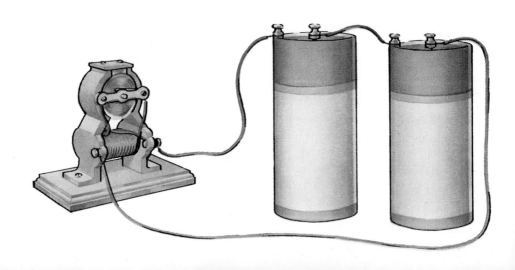

Make a list of ways that electric motors are used. Find pictures of machines that use electric motors and put them on your bulletin board.

A hundred years ago there were no electric motors. Much of the energy for machines came from the muscles of people and horses. Some of the energy came from wind and falling water. Some of it came from steam engines that burned wood and coal.

Electrical energy is easier to use than these other kinds of energy. It can be carried for miles in small wires. It is ready to be used the moment you touch a switch. There are no ashes and there is no smoke. There is little or no noise.

Think about some of our common machines, such as fans and washing machines. How would we make them run if there were no electricity?

Where Electricity Gets Its Energy

The electrical energy we use comes to us from machines called generators. As generators spin, they make electricity flow through wires. The generators are turned by water turbines or steam turbines. Thus you see that most of our electricity gets its energy from the energy of coal and falling water. The electrical energy is then changed in our homes and factories to other kinds of energy such as heat and the energy of moving things.

---

1. How many poles does an electromagnet have?
2. How can you change the strength of an electromagnet?
3. What happens when you change the direction of the electricity in an electromagnet?
4. What are some ways electromagnets are used?
5. Why is electricity so important today?
6. Where does most electrical energy come from?

Bird Study

Downy Woodpecker

Getting to Know Birds

Winter is a good time to begin the study of birds. Visit places where you can see winter birds. Become acquainted with as many kinds as you can before the spring birds come.

There are usually winter birds around feeding stations if plenty of food is kept in them. The best time to see the birds is in early morning when they are hungry.

Perhaps you would like to start a feeding station. Make a shelf or a tray on a post. Put a roof over it if you wish. Keep seeds and crumbs in the tray. Keep some beef fat under a piece of wire screen for the small, meat-eating birds.

Starling

English Sparrow

Purple Finch

Nuthatch

Other good places to look for winter birds are low bushes and tall weeds. Look in vacant lots at the edges of fields, along streams, and along roadsides. There are often birds in the bushes that are found in parks and around houses.

Crows, gulls, and many other birds go to places where garbage is dumped. Chickadees and woodpeckers are often seen in the woods.

When you see a new bird, read about it in a bird book. Find out what it eats. Find out whether it looks the same in the winter as in the summer. Find out where it lives in the summer.

203

Junco

Tree Sparrow

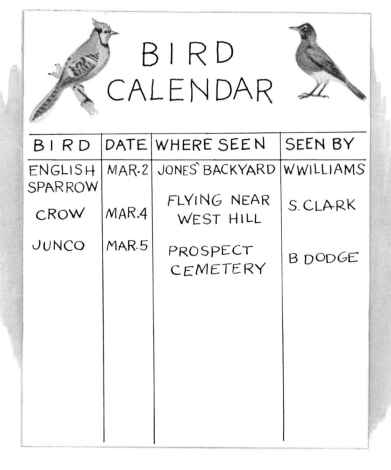

BIRD	DATE	WHERE SEEN	SEEN BY
ENGLISH SPARROW	MAR. 2	JONES' BACKYARD	W WILLIAMS
CROW	MAR. 4	FLYING NEAR WEST HILL	S. CLARK
JUNCO	MAR. 5	PROSPECT CEMETERY	B DODGE

Keeping Records

A good way to keep a record of the new birds you see
is to make a bird calendar. The whole class may have
a calendar. Each person may also have a calendar if
he wishes.

Write down the name of each new bird, where it was
seen, and the date it was first seen. You may also
wish to write down what the bird was doing.

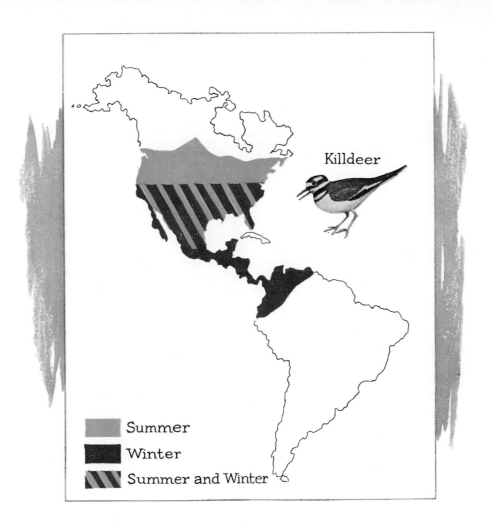

Killdeer

Summer

Winter

Summer and Winter

When you see a new bird, find out where it lives in the winter and where it lives in the summer. Most bird books will tell you this.

Then make a map like the one above. Use green for the places the bird lives in summer. Use red for the places it lives in winter. Make green lines and red lines in the places where the bird lives in both summer and winter.

Bird Nests

You can learn much about birds by studying their nests. The birds do not use their nests in winter so you can collect them then. The birds always build new nests in the spring.

Each time you find a nest, write down where you found it. Then try to find out the name of the bird that built the nest. Bird books and people who have studied birds can help you.

Make a picture of the bird that built the nest. Cut out the picture and put it with the nest. Do the same with other nests.

Take apart an old bird's nest. Sort the things it is made of and put them in different piles. Make a sign that tells where the nest was found and what bird made it.

You will find that some nests are made of twigs and bark. Some are made of grasses, tiny roots, and hair. Other nests are made of string, hair, and threads from plants. You will find thistle down in some nests and mud in others.

LEAVES

HAIR

SONG SPARROW NEST

BARK AND ROOTLETS

GRASS

Goldfinches

Female

Male

Male and Female Colors

You may see two birds that do not look alike building the same nest. You are probably looking at a male and a female bird.

Look at pictures of goldfinches, redwings, orioles, and tanagers. Notice that the males and females are so different that they do not seem to be the same kind of bird. Find pictures of other males and females that do not look alike. Look for them on your field trips.

Draw pictures of the males and females of some of these birds. Make a game with the pictures to see how many males and females you can put together correctly.

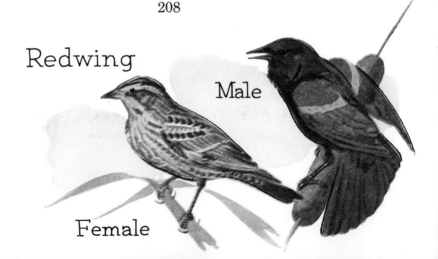

Redwing

Male

Female

English Sparrows

Female

Male

Female

Male

Downy Woodpeckers

Males and females of other kinds of birds look almost alike. You must look closely to see how they are different. A male English sparrow has a black bib and the female does not have one. The female kingfisher has a brown belt and the male does not have one.

The males and females of some kinds of birds look so much alike that you cannot tell them apart. You cannot tell a male crow from a female crow or a male song sparrow from a female song sparrow.

Learn the differences between the males and females of as many kinds of birds as you can. When you can tell them apart, write on your bird calendar the names of the ones you have seen.

Kingfishers

Male

Female

Making a Birdhouse

A birdhouse near your home will help you study birds. You can watch the birds day after day as they take care of their young.

You can make a good birdhouse from roofing paper and a few pieces of wood. First saw out a round piece of wood for the bottom of the house. Bore a small hole in the center of the wood for a nail. Then nail the piece of wood to the end of a long pole.

Cut a rectangle of roofing paper for the side of the house. Cut a hole in it for the door. Save the piece you cut out. Cut a circle of roofing paper for the roof of the birdhouse.

210

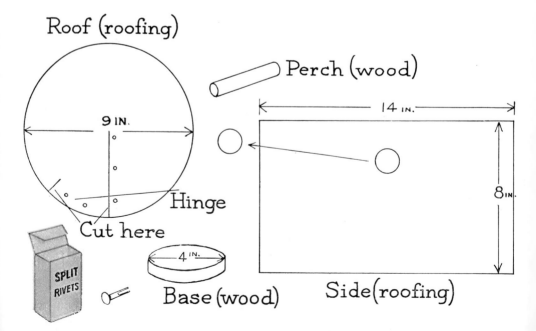

Roof (roofing)

Perch (wood)

9 IN.

Hinge

Cut here

SPLIT RIVETS

4 IN.

Base (wood)

14 IN.

8 IN.

Side (roofing)

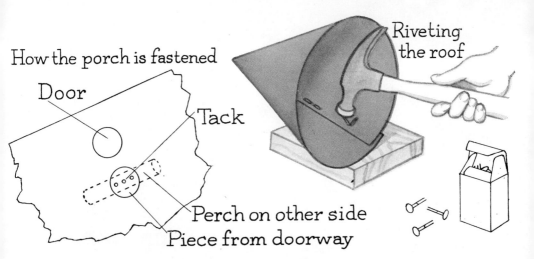

How the porch is fastened

Door

Tack

Riveting the roof

Perch on other side

Piece from doorway

Fasten the perch below the door with large tacks. Use the small piece of roofing paper from the doorway to strengthen the side where the tacks go through. The picture shows how to do this.

Form the roof into a cone and rivet it together. Then rivet the part of the roof marked "hinge" to the side of the house.

Roll the side of the house and rivet the edges together. The house should now look like the picture at the bottom of the page.

Nail the house to the round piece of wood that makes the bottom of the house. Use big-headed nails.

A good place for the house is a garden or a field where it will be shaded during the middle of the day.

211

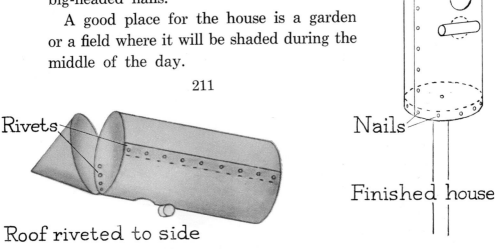

Rivets

Roof riveted to side

Nails

Finished house

Territories

Many male birds set up territories for nesting and feeding. Then each male tries to keep other males out of his territory.

A male song sparrow chooses for his territory a place where there are shrubs, small trees, and thickets. He goes to the center of his territory and begins to sing. The song seems to be a warning for other male song sparrows to stay out.

If another male comes into his territory, the first male tries to drive him out. They may fight. The first male usually wins, but sometimes he loses his territory.

Look for a song sparrow singing in the top of a shrub or a small tree. This is a male. Listen to find out if other males start to sing when the first one sings. Watch him to see if he drives away other song sparrows.

If a song sparrow sets up a territory near your home, try to find out how big his territory is. Make a map. Mark on the map the places where the song sparrow does most of his singing.

Watch the song sparrow drive away other males. Notice where he stops chasing them. You will soon be able to draw a line on your map to show where his territory is.

213

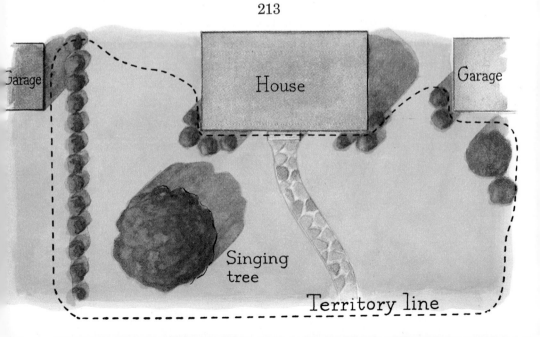

Garage

House

Garage

Singing
tree

Territory line

Flight feather   Covering feather   Fluff feather

Feathers

Look at different kinds of feathers. Notice the stiff feathers from the wing of a bird. How does a bird use these feathers? Notice the feathers that cover the bird as shingles cover a house. Pour some drops of water on them and note what happens. Look for the fluffy feathers that keep the bird warm.

Notice how light feathers are. Why is this helpful to a flying bird? Notice the way feathers are made. Perhaps you can look at a feather under a microscope and see the tiny hooks that hold the stiff parts together.

214

Hen

Get the feathers of a large bird such as a hen or a rooster. Pick out the wing feathers and the tail feathers. Pick out some of the covering feathers. Then make a life-size drawing of the bird and glue the different feathers in the proper places on the drawing.

You may find some bird feathers. Bring them in and make a chart like the one above for each kind of bird.

Going down   Going up

Bird Flight

Wave a large wing feather downward. Notice how the air pushes up on the feather. Now wave the feather upward without turning it over. Notice how easily the feather moves. The air slips past it easily.

When a bird moves its wings downward, the air pushes up on the feathers. This makes the bird rise. When the wings go up again, the air slips easily between the feathers.

Take the feathers from a dead bird's wing. Mount them on a chart that shows how the feathers are arranged in a wing.

216

Wing of pigeon

Up again

Down again

Watch birds flying. Notice that different kinds of birds have different ways of flying. Some move their wings rapidly and some move them slowly. Some flap their wings two or three times, glide a few feet, and then flap their wings again.

Some gulls and hawks have light bodies and large wings. They do not flap their wings as often as heavier birds do. At times you may see them soar without flapping their wings at all.

Most birds use their tails to help steer themselves during quick turns. They also use their tails to keep themselves balanced. They often use them to slow their speed before landing. Watch a pigeon as it lands and notice the way it uses its tail.

217

Pigeon landing

Wing muscles

The biggest muscles in most birds are the muscles that flap the wings downward. These muscles are in the breast of the bird. Have you noticed that most of the meat of a chicken is in the breast? The breast meat of a chicken is made up of wing muscles.

A bird's wings are much like your arms and have many of the same muscles. Pretend one of your arms is a wing. Push it down against a table top and feel your chest with your other hand. Find the muscles that become hard. Muscles like these pull a bird's wing down.

Bring the bones of a chicken or a turkey to school. Clean them by boiling them in soap and water.

Try to find some of the same bones in this picture. Which ones are somewhat like the bones in your own body?

Find the breast bone. A bird needs a big breast bone to hold the wing muscles. Find your own breast bone. How is it different?

The "wishbone" is somewhat like your collarbone, but it is large and strong compared with the other bones. It helps hold the wing muscles.

Heavy bones would make it hard for a bird to fly. Break open the leg bone of a chicken. Notice that it is hollow. How does this help a bird?

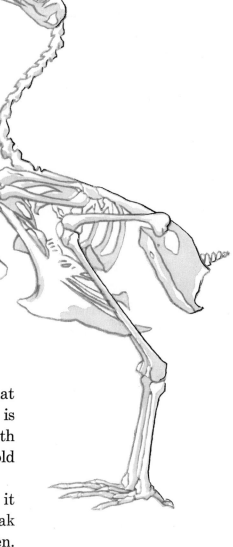

219

Leg bone of hen

White spot

Birds' Eggs

Look at the yolk of a hen's egg. You will see a little white spot on one side. This is the part of the egg that grows into a chicken. The yolk and the white are the food for the growing chicken.

Many birds lay an egg a day until there are four eggs in the nest. Hummingbirds stop when there are two eggs. Hens and ducks may lay ten or more eggs.

Eggs begin to grow in a long tube inside the female bird. The white spot and the yolk are formed at the upper end of the tube. As the egg moves along the tube, glands add first the white and then the shell. Then the egg is laid in the nest.

White spot
and yolk
formed here

White added here

Shell added here

The female bird keeps the eggs dry and warm with her own body. The male bird may help her, but the males of many kinds of birds such as ducks and chickens do not help take care of the eggs or the young.

The white spot soon begins to grow. At first it does not look much like a bird. The heart and blood can be seen first. Then the head begins to show.

Later the eyes show and the legs and wings begin to grow. After two or three weeks the bird is fully formed. Then it picks a hole in the shell and comes out.

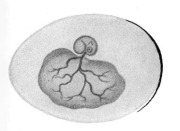

Baby robin

The Care of Young Birds

Many kinds of young birds are help-
less when they hatch. They are blind
and they cannot walk. They have no
feathers. They need much care before
they are ready to leave the nest.

The mother bird keeps them warm and dry. She
stays on the nest at night and during rains. During
most of the day she hunts food for them. The males
of some kinds of birds help take care of the young.

Watch a nest of young birds. Notice how often the
parent birds bring food. Use a watch and a notebook to
keep a record for a report to the class.

Female robin
and young robins

Baby bobwhite

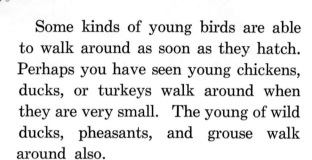

Some kinds of young birds are able to walk around as soon as they hatch. Perhaps you have seen young chickens, ducks, or turkeys walk around when they are very small. The young of wild ducks, pheasants, and grouse walk around also.

These young birds usually spend a longer time in the eggs. When they hatch they are covered with down. Their eyes are open. They can feed themselves.

The female bird leads her young birds to places where they can find food. She keeps them warm and dry at night. She tries to keep them from danger.

223

Female grouse and young

Cowbirds

Cowbirds do not build nests. The females do not take care of their eggs or their young. Yet there are always many cowbirds.

The females lay their eggs in the nests of other birds. These other birds take care of the cowbirds' eggs and young along with their own. You will be interested in reading more about the habits of cowbirds.

———

1. Name some birds that live near your home all through the year.
2. Name some birds that live near your home only in summer.
3. Tell how some kinds of young birds look when they hatch.
4. Which muscles are biggest in most birds?
5. How are feathers useful to birds?
6. Explain how you can tell the difference between some male and female birds.

How Airplanes Fly

Controlling an Airplane

This is the pilot's cabin of a small airplane. Look at the pedals and the wheel that the pilot uses to control the plane.

He steers the plane with the pedals. He pulls or pushes on the wheel to make the plane climb or dive. He turns the wheel to make the plane tip.

On the next page a plane is turning, climbing, and diving. Tell what the pilot uses to make it do each of these things.

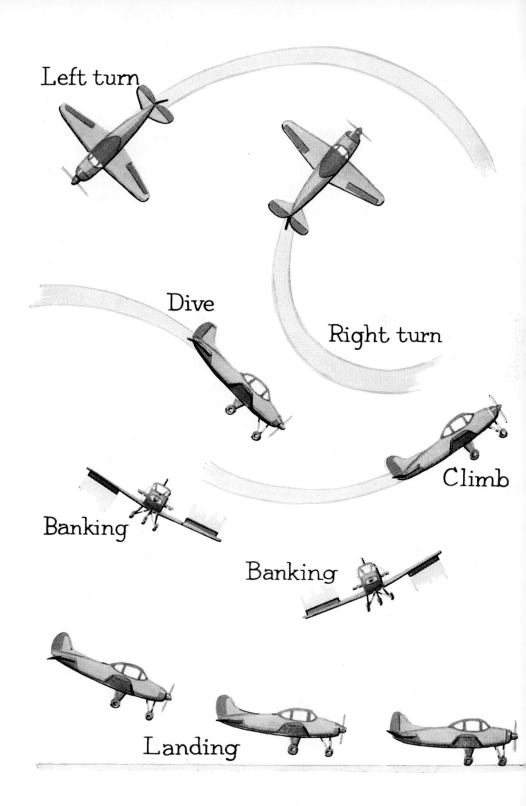

Left turn

Right turn

Dive

Climb

Banking

Banking

Landing

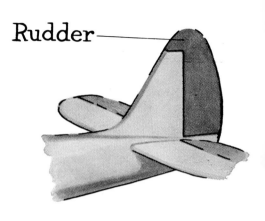

Rudder

Steering a Plane

The rudder of an air-
plane makes the plane
turn to the right or to the
left. It is part of the tail
of the plane.

Cut a piece of light cardboard in the shape of an
airplane. Glue an upright piece of cardboard to the
tail of the plane as shown in the picture below. The
back of the upright piece will be the rudder.

Find the balancing point of the model. Push a pin
through this point into the cork of a bottle.

Blow through a soda straw at the model plane. Bend
the rudder to the left and blow at the model. Bend the
rudder to the right and blow at the model. What happens each time?

Soda straw

Pin

Glue here

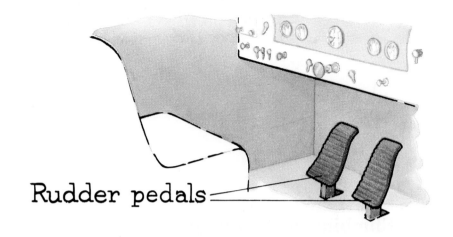

Rudder pedals

A pilot steers his airplane with his feet. There are two pedals in front of him. He pushes on the right pedal to make the plane turn right. He pushes on the left pedal to make the plane turn left.

A push on the right pedal turns the rudder to the right. The wind now presses on the rudder and swings the tail of the plane so that it turns to the right.

Explain why pushing on the left pedal makes the plane turn to the left.

229

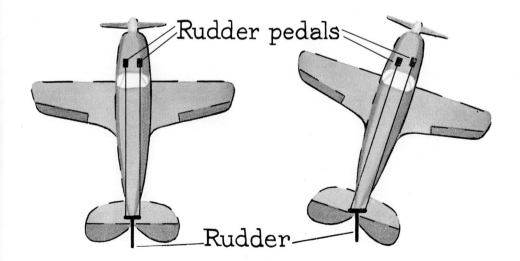

Rudder pedals

Rudder

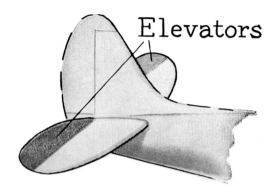

Elevators

Climbing and Diving

The elevators are used to make an airplane climb and dive. The elevators are part of the tail of a plane.

Cut some thin cardboard in the shape of the piece shown below. Cut another piece just like it. Bend over the tail pieces and glue the rest of the cardboard together.

Find the balancing point of this model. Push a pin through this point into a cork in a bottle. Bend the elevators up and blow through a straw at the model. Bend the elevators down and blow at it again.

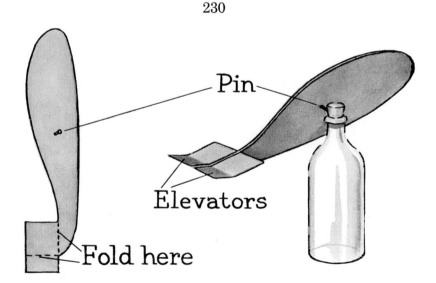

Pin

Elevators

Fold here

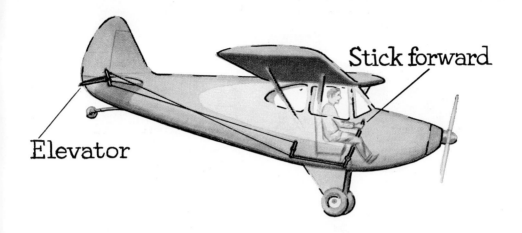

Stick forward

Elevator

In some planes the pilot moves the elevators by pulling or pushing a wheel in front of him. In other planes, the pilot pulls or pushes a lever, called the "stick."

The pilot turns the elevators down by pushing on the wheel or the stick. The wind then pushes up against the elevators and pushes the tail up. The plane is now heading downward.

The pilot turns the elevators up by pulling on the wheel or the stick. When the elevators turn up, the wind presses against them. This pushes the back of the plane down and makes it head upward.

231

Stick back

Elevator

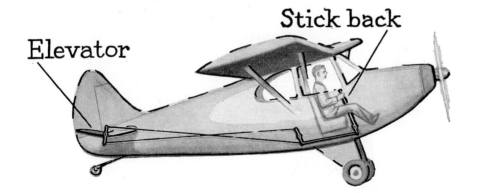

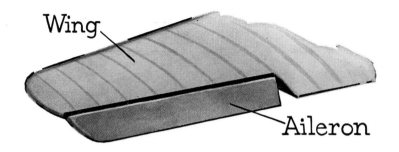

Wing

Aileron

Making a Plane Bank

The ailerons are on the ends of the wings. When one aileron is turned down, the other aileron is turned up. The ailerons can bank the airplane to one side or the other, and they can make the plane fly level again.

Cut some thin cardboard in the shape of a plane. Make a cut in the back of each wing so that you can bend a piece of the wing up and down as an aileron.

Fasten a thread to the nose of the model. Pull the model straight up slowly. Now bend one aileron up and the other aileron down. Pull the model up slowly again. What happens each time?

232

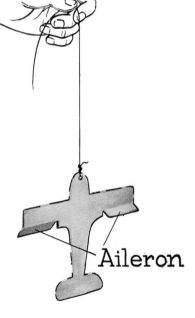

Aileron

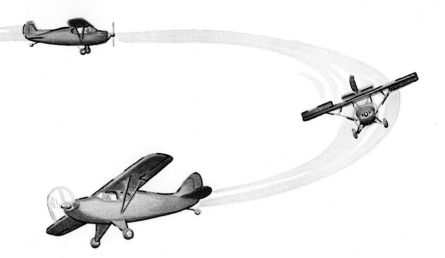

Have you noticed that roads are often banked on
curves? This is so that automobiles do not slide off
when they turn at high speed. Airplanes must be
banked also so that they do not slip on turns.

The ailerons are moved by the stick or the control
wheel. When a pilot pushes the stick or turns the
wheel to the right, the left aileron goes down and the
right aileron goes up. The wind now pushes down on
the right aileron and up on the left aileron. That makes
the plane bank to the right.

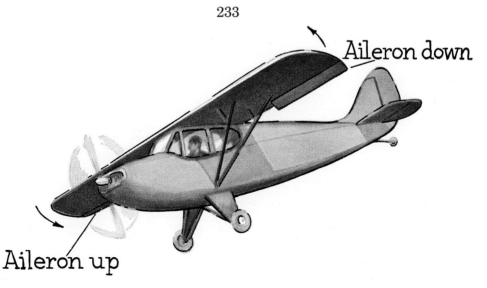

Aileron down

Aileron up

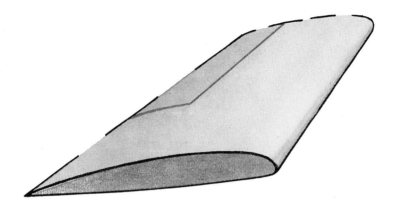

An Airplane Wing

Some of the first airplane wings were flat. Years of experiments, however, have given us the shape of the wings we see on planes today. The modern airplane wing is curved on the top and nearly flat on the bottom; it is thin at the rear edge and thick near the front.

As the wing goes through the air, the air separates. Part of the air goes under the wing. Part of it goes over. It has been discovered that both the air over the wing and the air under the wing help to raise the wing.

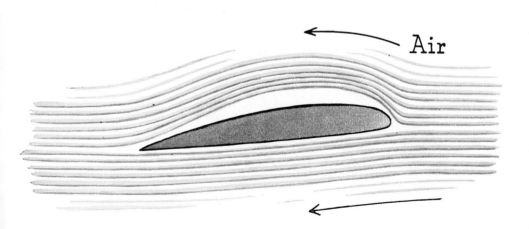

Air

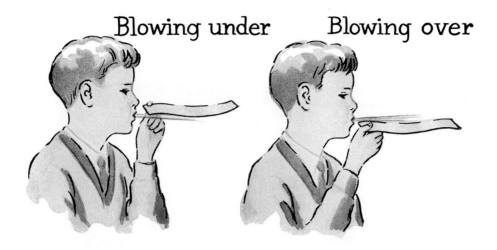

Blowing under   Blowing over

Put one end of a strip of paper against your upper lip and blow. What happens? Put the end of the strip against your lower lip and blow. What happens? Notice that air blowing over the paper raises the paper just as blowing under it does.

Lay a card on one end of a ruler. Use thumbtacks to fasten another card on the first one so that the upper card is curved. Balance the ruler on your thumb. Blow over the curved card. What happens?

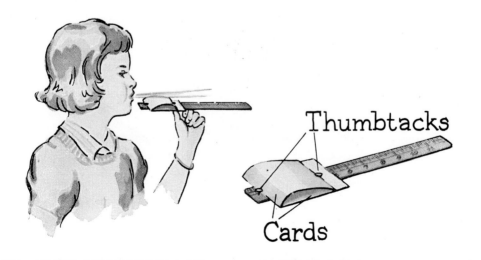

Thumbtacks

Cards

Making Airplanes Move

All planes except jets and gliders use propellers. A propeller is something like an electric fan. There is a twist in each blade of a propeller. The propeller pushes back on the air as it turns.

Put a board on three round pencils on a table. Put an electric fan on the board. Turn on the fan and notice what happens.

As the air is pushed in one direction, the fan is pushed in the other. Airplanes are moved forward by the propellers in much the same way.

236

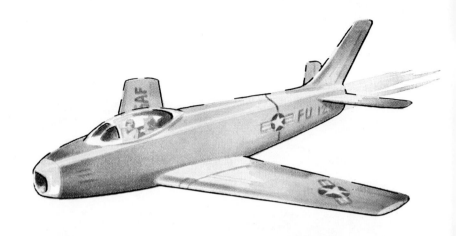

There are planes that have no propellers. Some are jet planes. Jet planes fly much faster than planes with propellers.

To understand how a jet plane moves, blow up a rubber balloon. Then let go of the balloon and watch it.

Air rushes out the mouth of the balloon. This moving air pushes back on the balloon. The push makes the balloon fly about until the air is gone.

In jet planes, hot gases from burning fuel rush from openings in the planes. The push of these gases drives the planes ahead.

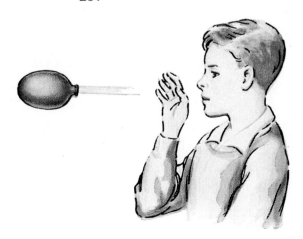

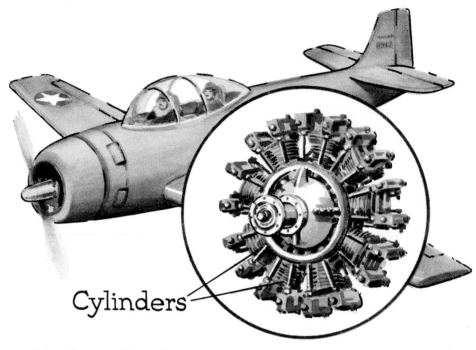

Cylinders

Airplane Engines

Propeller-driven planes use gasoline engines. These engines work much like the gasoline engines in automobiles.

There are two or more cylinders in an airplane engine. Big engines have many cylinders.

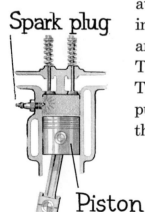

Spark plug

A cylinder is closed at one end and open at the other. A piston slides back and forth in the cylinder. Gasoline vapor and air are pumped into the cylinders of the engine. They are set on fire with an electric spark. The air becomes hot and grows bigger. It pushes on the pistons and makes a force that turns the propellers.

238

Piston

Jet engines have only a few moving parts. Air is pumped into the front of the engine by a rapidly whirling fan. This air is mixed with the fuel. The fuel burns and heats the air to a high temperature.

The air becomes much bigger as it is heated, and it rushes out the back of the engine with great force. This rushing air is called the jet. On its way out, the rapidly moving air spins a turbine that drives the air pump at the front of the engine.

Jet engines drive planes very rapidly, but they use more fuel than planes with gasoline engines. They also need longer runways for landing and taking off.

239

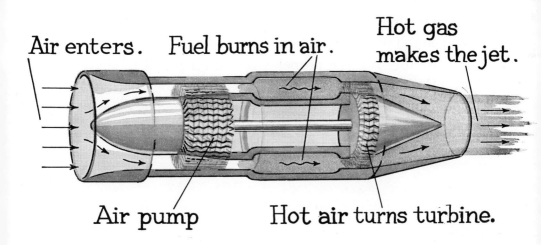

Air enters.   Fuel burns in air.   Hot gas makes the jet.

Air pump   Hot air turns turbine.

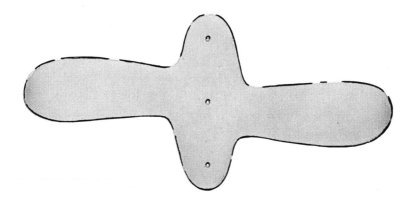

Making a Propeller

Lay a sheet of thin paper on the above outline. Trace the outline. Then use carbon paper to make the same outline on thin cardboard. Cut around the outline and punch three holes in it as shown.

Carefully roll the propeller around a pencil to shape it. Roll it until the three holes come together. As you can see in the picture below, one edge of each blade is curved and the other edge is flat.

Straighten out a paper clip for the propeller shaft. Push it through the three holes in the propeller. Find three glass beads and slip them on the wire for bearings. Bend one end of the wire around the propeller. Bend a hook in the other end of the wire.

Make a small hole in the end of a soap box and push the propeller shaft through it. Slip three rubber bands over a pencil and hook them to the propeller shaft.

Set the box on some round pencils. Wind up the propeller and then let it go.

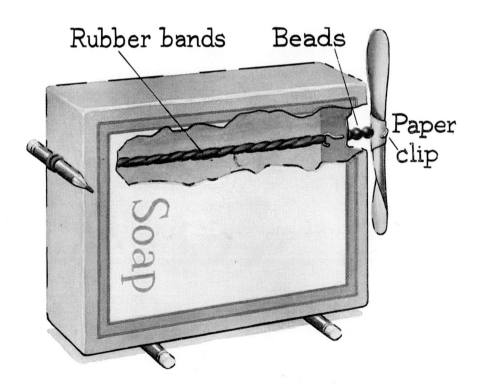

Rubber bands   Beads   Paper clip

Soap

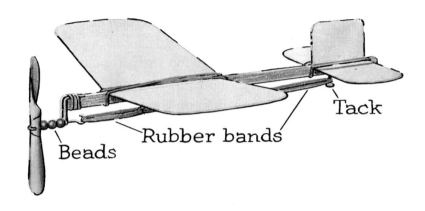

Tack

Rubber bands

Beads

A Flying Model

This flying model will help you understand more about how airplanes fly. It uses the propeller and the rubber band motor that you just made.

You will need a stick of balsa wood 12 inches long and one-fourth inch square. Balsa wood is very light. You can buy it in stores that sell things for making models.

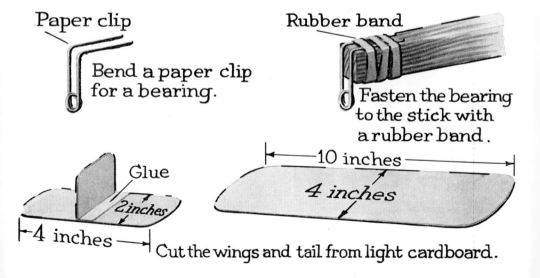

Paper clip

Bend a paper clip for a bearing.

Rubber band

Fasten the bearing to the stick with a rubber band.

Glue

2 inches

4 inches

10 inches

4 inches

Cut the wings and tail from light cardboard.

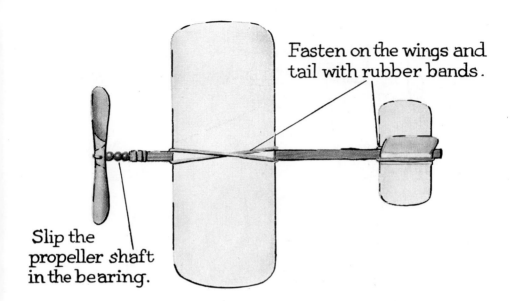

Fasten on the wings and tail with rubber bands.

Slip the propeller shaft in the bearing.

Put the model together as shown on these two pages. Be sure that the wings are slanted as shown at the top of page 242.

Turn the propeller backward about 100 turns with your finger. Give the plane a gentle push forward and let it go.

If the plane noses up or down too much, move the wings backward or forward a little.

You can buy kits for making other kinds of model planes. Some of them help you to make wings that have more lift than the flat wings on this model have.

243

Air Resistance

Wave a piece of cardboard with its flat side to the front. Notice the air resistance. Then wave the cardboard with its edge to the front. Notice the difference.

There is always air resistance when you move anything through the air. This is because you must push the air out of the way. When you waved the cardboard, you had to move much air the first time and only a little air the second time.

Try moving the cardboard rapidly and then again slowly. Which way makes more air resistance? Have you noticed any differences in air resistance when you rode on a bicycle?

Air resistance can be very great when airplanes move hundreds of miles an hour. Men who plan airplanes try countless experiments to find ways of keeping air resistance as small as possible.

Experiments have shown that the best shape is that shown above. Study the pictures of airplanes and notice how close the planes come to this shape. What did the builders do with the motors, the wings, and the tail to keep air resistance low? What did they do with the landing wheels?

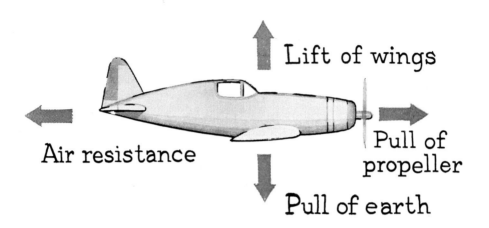

Lift of wings

Air resistance

Pull of propeller

Pull of earth

Forces on an Airplane

There are four big forces that act on an airplane. The earth pulls downward on an airplane. The wings lift the plane. The propeller pulls it forward. Air resistance holds it back.

The diagram below shows a plane just after the pilot made the engine turn faster. The pull of the propeller is now greater than the air resistance. The airplane will begin to move faster.

246

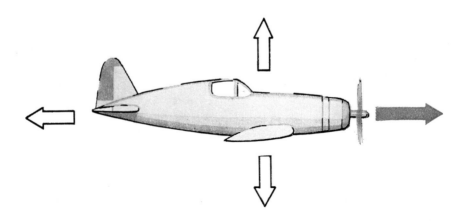

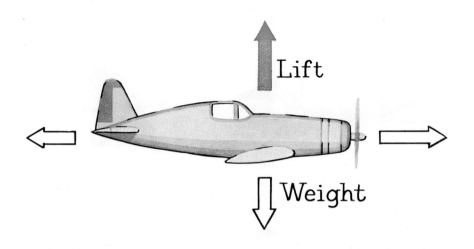

In the upper diagram on this page, the lift of the wings is greater because the airplane is going faster. The plane will now rise. When a pilot takes off from an airfield, he wants the airplane to go as fast as it can so the lift will be much greater than the weight.

In the diagram below, the lift of the wings is small because the airplane is going slowly. The lift is less than the weight. The plane will drop slowly as it moves along.

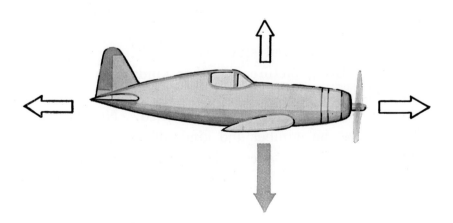

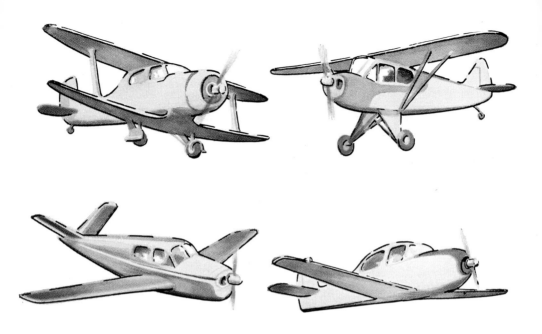

Kinds of Airplanes

People have experimented with many different kinds of planes. No one plane has been discovered to be perfect for every use. Some kinds are cheap to build, but they cannot carry heavy loads. Some kinds fly very fast, but they need long runways for landing and taking off.

Visit an airfield and study some different kinds of airplanes. Bring pictures of other kinds of airplanes to school.

Notice where the wings are fastened. Notice the tail. Notice the number and kinds of engines. Look for ways the air resistance is kept as small as possible.

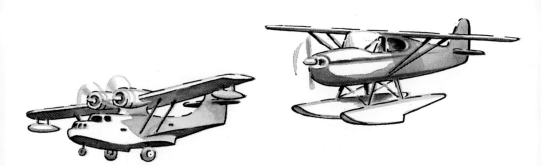

Most airplanes have landing wheels for landing on and taking off from the ground. Some airplanes, however, can land on and take off from the water.

Many of these planes are small. They have floats under the body and the wings. The bodies of the bigger planes are often built like boats. These planes can land and take off from large bodies of water where there are big waves.

There are uses for airplanes that can land on either the water or the ground. These planes have both floats and wheels. They are called amphibian planes.

Helicopters

A helicopter has wings that spin around, something like a propeller. When they spin rapidly, they pull the helicopter straight up. When they spin slowly, the helicopter sinks downward. There is also a small propeller on the tail that keeps the helicopter from turning around and around. How are helicopters used?

---

1. What causes the upward force on an airplane wing?
2. What does the propeller do?
3. What forces act on a plane while it is flying?
4. What makes a jet plane fly?
5. How does a pilot bank his plane as he makes a turn?
6. What are the elevators of an airplane used for?
7. How is the air resistance of a plane kept small?

Warm Air in Motion

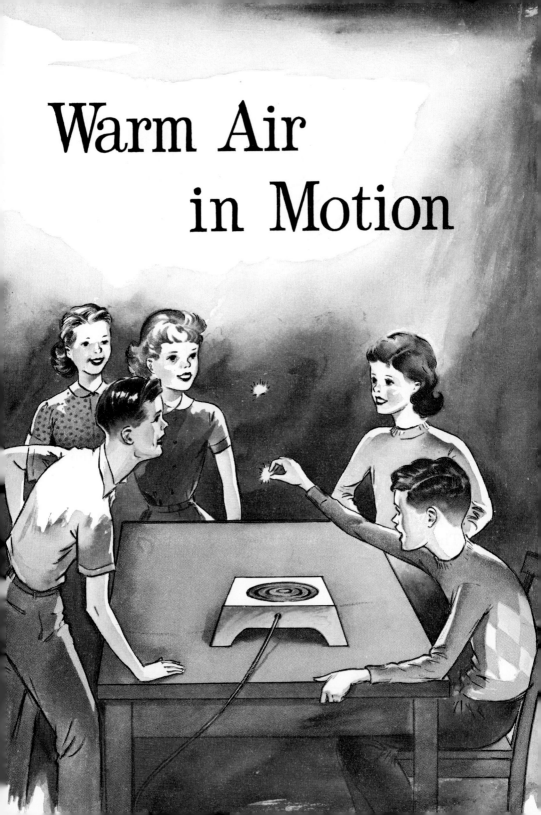

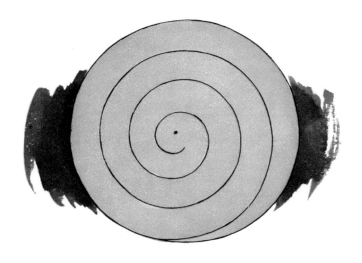

A Whirling Spiral

Draw a spiral like this one on a sheet of heavy paper. Cut along the line from the outside to the center. Push a knotted thread through the center hole.

Lift the spiral by the thread. It should spread out evenly like the one in the picture below. If it does not hang evenly, you may have made the lines too close together or too far apart. Try again until you have a good spiral.

Hold the spiral over your head and blow through it. The spiral should turn as the air moves up through it.

252

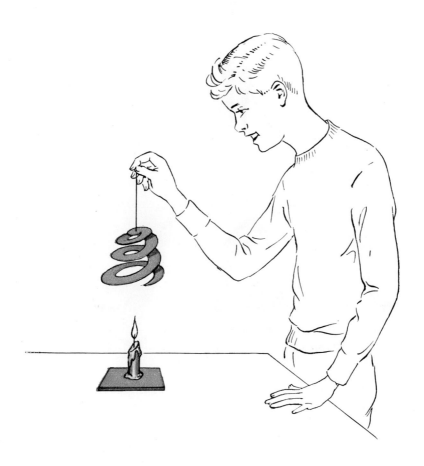

Hold the spiral over an unlighted candle. Then hold it over a lighted candle, being careful not to let the paper come too close to the flame.

Hold the spiral over an electric hot plate. Turn on the electricity and notice what happens as the hot plate becomes heated.

The spiral spins when it is in heated air. It is turned by the rising air.

Warm Air in a Tepee

Indians who live in tepees know how air moves when it is warmed. They build their fire in the center of a tepee. They leave an opening at the top for the smoke to go out.

Cold air comes in around the bottom of the tepee. The air is warmed by the fire and rises, taking the smoke with it. This smoky warm air goes out the top of the tepee.

Indians usually sit or squat in a tepee while a fire is burning. The air near the ground has less smoke in it than the air higher up.

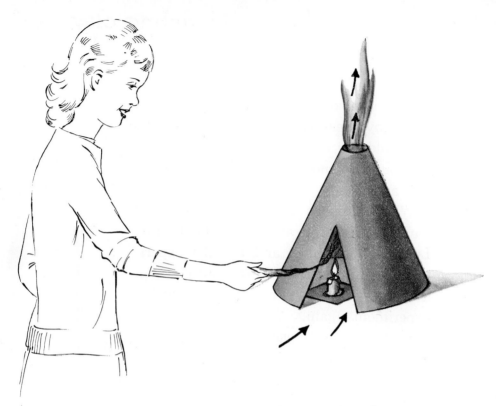

Make a little tepee from a sheet of paper and some sticky tape. Use a very short candle in the tepee for the fire. Keep the candle in the middle of the tepee so that there is less danger from fire.

Hold your hand over the tepee. Can you feel warm air coming out?

Roll up a sheet of tissue paper. Light the paper, let it burn a few seconds, and then blow out the flame. The tissue will give off smoke.

Hold the smoking paper near the opening at the bottom of the tepee. Where does the smoke go? Is the air smoky inside the tepee? Describe the path of the air in the tepee.

Modeling clay

What Heating Does to Air

Fasten a soda straw in the neck of a bottle by pressing modeling clay around it. Hold the bottle between your hands and put the end of the straw in a glass of water.

What happens as the heat of your hands warms the air inside the bottle? Let the bottle cool and try the experiment again. Put the bottle outdoors on a cold day until it is cold. Then try the experiment again. What happens?

256

Open two paper bags, turn them upside down, and tie them to the ends of a yardstick. Balance the yardstick on a round pencil.

Heat the air in one of the bags with an electric lamp or a candle flame. You must hold the bag with one hand so that it will not be pushed upward by the rising air.

After a few moments of heating, take away the lamp and let go of the bag. What happens? What happens after the bag cools again?

Try the experiment several times, heating first one bag and then the other. Which seems to be heavier, a bag of warm air or a bag of cool air?

Why Heated Air Rises

Your experiments have shown that air expands and thus takes up more space as it is heated. Let us study the last experiment to see why the air becomes lighter when it is heated.

At the beginning of the experiment, the air in both bags has the same temperature and both bags weigh the same. When you heated the air in one bag, the air expanded and some of it left the bag. This bag then weighed less than the other because there was less air in it.

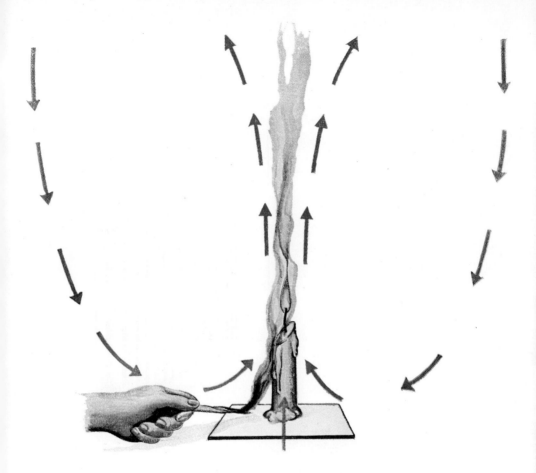

Air around a candle rises for the same reason the bag of warm air rose in the last experiment. The air over the candle flame is heated and expands. This air then weighs less than the cool air above it. In other words, the earth pulls harder on cool air than it does on warm air.

The cool air moves down and pushes the warm air up out of its way. Some of the cool air near the flame is now heated and is pushed up in its turn. A steady flow of air is set up.

259

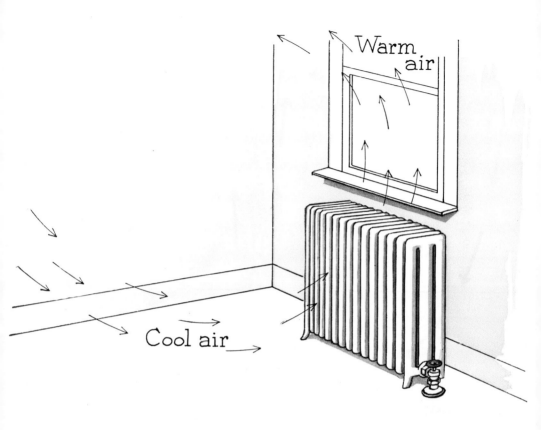

Warm air

Cool air

Using the Movement of Heated Air

A radiator on one side of a room can heat other parts of a room. Air near the radiator is warmed and expands. Cool air above it moves down and pushes the warm air up. Tell what happens next.

Where would you expect the warmest place in the room to be? Where would you expect to find the coolest air? Hang thermometers in different parts of the room and find the temperatures of the air in these places.

Cool air

Warm air inside a chimney weighs less than cool air outdoors. The cool air enters the house through cracks and keyholes and pushes the warm air up the chimney. Why does this make the fire burn more brightly?

Can you explain why there is a draft in a stove or furnace?

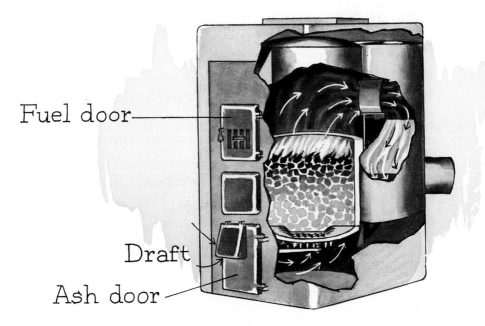

Fuel door

Draft

Ash door

Sunlight

Unequal Heating of Surfaces

Lay a sheet of dark paper and a sheet of white paper on a sunny window sill. After a few minutes, touch the dark paper and the white paper. Which feels warmer?

Try the experiment with dark cloth and white cloth. Try it with white sand and dark sand.

Sunlight warms things it falls upon. The white paper reflects much of the sunlight. The dark paper changes much of the sunlight into heat.

Sunlight

Dry soil

Water

Set a dish of water and a dish of dry soil on a sunny window sill. After half an hour, hold your hand over the soil and then over the water. Which seems warmer?

Water does not heat up so rapidly as soil when sunlight falls on it. More of the sunlight is reflected from the water. The water also needs more energy than soil needs to make it change temperature.

263

Go outdoors on a sunny day and touch different things. Touch the shiny parts of an automobile and the painted parts. Which parts are hotter, or are they both the same?

Does a concrete walk or the grass growing beside it seem to be the hotter? Does bare ground or grass-covered ground become hotter?

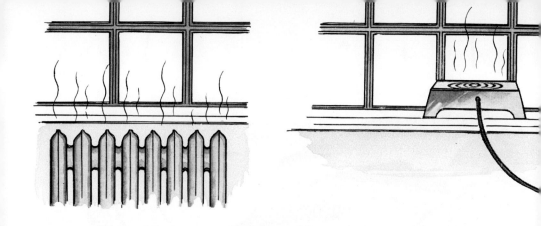

Look at a heated radiator or a hot plate that is in sunlight. Notice how things beyond them seem to dance about. Place a lighted candle in sunlight and notice its shadow. Notice that there are wavy lines around the flame.

Light bends when it enters and leaves warm air just as it bends when it enters and leaves glass. Air over something hot becomes heated and rises. Light going through this rising air is bent more or less as the air moves about.

You can see somewhat the same thing outdoors on a hot sunny day. The sunlight heats solid things like sidewalks and roads. The air next to the solid things is heated and rises. When you look through the heated air, things seem to dance and wave about.

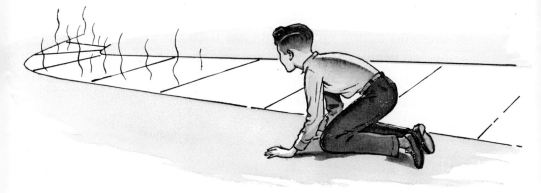

Rising and Falling Air Currents

Sunshine heats land faster than it heats water. The air above land becomes warmer than the air above lakes. Cool air above lakes moves down toward the land and pushes the warm air up. You say that a breeze is blowing when you feel the air move from the cool places to the warm places.

The sun does not heat all parts of the land equally. Rising and falling air currents are found over different kinds of fields. Which do you think is hotter on a sunny day, a bare field or a grass-covered field? Make up an experiment to test your answer.

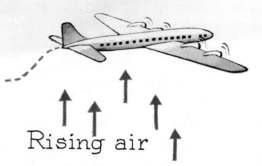

Rising air

Airplane passengers often have bumpy rides on sunny afternoons. As a plane moves through rising air currents, it is raised a bit by each of them. As it moves through downward currents, it is carried downward a little.

Planes travel so fast they are not carried up and down very far by little currents of air. The planes are just shaken up a bit. If they get in large currents, they may be carried up or down a long way.

Flying is less bumpy high from the ground because the rising air currents cool off before they get very high. Airplanes fly above these currents as much as possible. Why do you think flying is less bumpy on cloudy days and at night than it is on sunny afternoons?

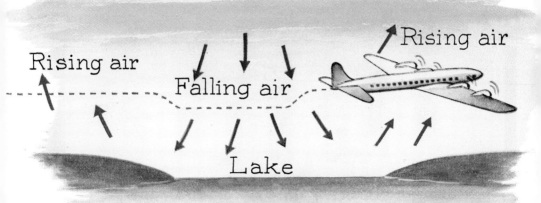

Rising air

Rising air

Falling air

Lake

Warm air   Cool air

Breezes Along the Shore

Your experiments have shown that soil heats up faster than water. Study the picture above and you will see why there is often a breeze blowing from the water toward the land on sunny afternoons in summer.

As the sun sets, the land cools quickly. The land soon becomes as cool as the water. Then the air over the land has the same temperature as the air over the water. The breeze stops blowing.

During the night, the land may become cooler than the water. The air over the land then becomes cool, too. Cool air from the land moves over the shore and pushes up the warmer air over the water.

When morning comes, the sun warms the land again. When the air over the land has the same temperature as the air over the water, the breeze stops again. Notice the way the breezes blow next summer if you go to the shore of the ocean or a large lake.

269

Rising Air and Clouds

Rising air cools as it goes up. Sometimes it holds much water vapor. The water vapor condenses into tiny drops of water as the air cools.

Cumulus clouds form in this way. The bottom of a cumulus cloud shows where the air is cold enough to make the water vapor condense.

Look for cumulus clouds on sunny days. Imagine that you can see the rising air currents that make the clouds. If you were an airplane pilot, what would you expect to happen as you flew under a cumulus cloud?

Sunrise

Midmorning

Midafternoon

Sunset

Perhaps you have known days like this one. Cumulus clouds begin to form in the late morning after the land heats up in sunlight. As more warm air rises during the hot afternoon, there are more and larger clouds. When the soil cools again near sunset, warm air stops rising, the cumulus clouds evaporate, and the sky is clear again.

Ice crystals

Tiny drops of water

Thunderstorms

Thunderstorms are most common on hot afternoons in summer. The air is often hot and moist on such afternoons. Rising air currents build up tall cumulus clouds.

The tops of these big clouds may be so high that they are above the freezing level. The tops of such clouds are made up of ice crystals. We call these big clouds "thunderheads."

272

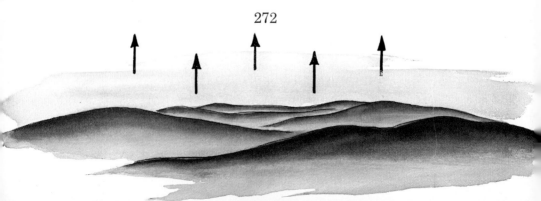

Cold air   Hot air   Cold air

The rising air currents that make a thunderhead may move faster and faster. Sometimes they may rise faster than a hundred miles an hour. At the same time, the storm begins to move across the country.

Ice crystals from the tops of the clouds are blown down into the warm air beneath. Water vapor condenses on these cold crystals. They may become big enough to fall. Sometimes the drops are caught in currents of falling air and blown against the ground with great force.

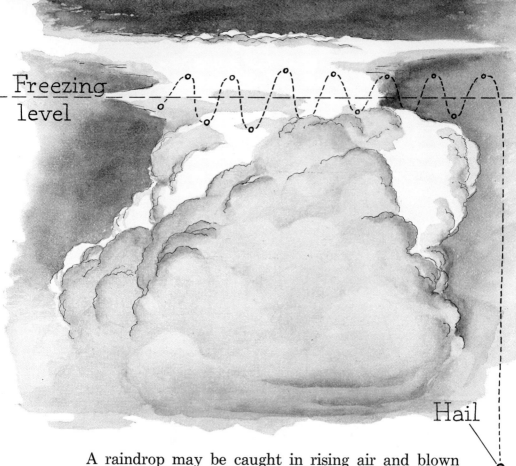

Freezing level

Hail

A raindrop may be caught in rising air and blown high enough to freeze. Then when it falls into warm moist air again, water vapor condenses on it and makes it bigger. If the drop is blown up above the freezing level several times, it may become a large piece of hail.

Hail is sometimes blown to the ground with great force. A hail storm may break windows, dent automobiles, knock fruit from trees, and cut off garden plants.

If a hailstone is cut open, it usually shows the layers of ice that were formed as it was blown up and down in the thunderhead.

We believe that electric charges are formed when raindrops are blown apart by swift air currents in a thunderhead. One kind of charge is formed on the smaller parts of the raindrops. The other kind of charge is formed on the larger parts of the raindrops.

The smaller parts are carried higher than the larger parts. Soon the top of the thunderhead has many charges of one kind, and other parts of the cloud have charges of the other kind. A spark jumps from one part of the cloud to another. Sometimes a spark jumps from one part of the cloud to the ground.

This spark which we call lightning heats the air around it. The air expands suddenly and sends out vibrations in all directions. The vibrations cause the sound we call thunder.

275

Tornadoes

Rapidly rising air currents may begin to spin as they rise. They spin faster and faster until the wind may go over 500 miles an hour. If one of these storms passes over buildings and crops it does great damage. Fortunately, these storms are small and do not last long. They are not common in most parts of the country.

---

1. What happens to air when it is heated?
2. Why does heated air rise when it is free to do so?
3. Where can you find heated air moving in homes?
4. Where might a pilot expect to find rapidly rising currents of air?
5. How are cumulus clouds formed?
6. What is a thunderhead?
7. Why is there often a breeze at the shore on sunny days in summer?

Water
in the Ground

Where Rain Water Goes

Thousands of gallons of water may fall on a field during one rain storm. Part of this water evaporates into the air again. Part of it runs away in streams. The rest of the water soaks into the soil.

278

The water that evaporates is gone. It has done us little good. The water that runs away is also gone. If it runs away too rapidly, it may do harm by carrying away soil and perhaps causing floods.

The water that soaks into the ground is useful. Plants use it. People and animals drink it from springs and wells. The water that is left flows slowly from springs into streams where it keeps fish alive, turns water wheels, and floats boats.

279

Testing Soil Drainage

Water passes through some kinds of soil more rapidly than through other kinds of soil.

Punch several small nail holes in the bottoms of two metal cans. Fill one can about three-quarters full with dry sand and the other with dry clay. Set the cans on glass jars to catch the water that drips from them.

Pour the same amount of water into each can. Which soil lets the water go through faster? Try other kinds of soil.

280

This experiment shows the effect of decayed plants on the moisture in soil. Fill one of the two cans with dry humus from the woods or with dry peat moss. Fill the other can with sand.

Pour the same amount of water into each can. What happens? Does humus help soil hold more or less water? How do forests help keep water in the soil?

281

The Water Level in Soil

Water that goes into soil may fill the spaces in the soil. A model will show how this happens.

Put sand in an aquarium as shown in the picture. Sprinkle water on the sand. Watch it pass through the sand and fill up the space in the sand at the bottom.

Dig a well near one side of the aquarium using a stick. Put a glass tube in the hole. Now you can see how water goes into a well.

Some of the water will evaporate from the sand during the next few days. Notice that the water level becomes lower in the sand and in the well. Another sprinkling will bring it back to the first level.

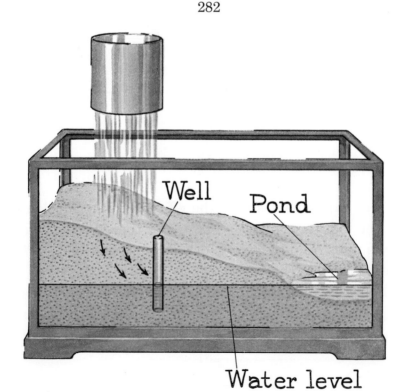

Well

Pond

Water level

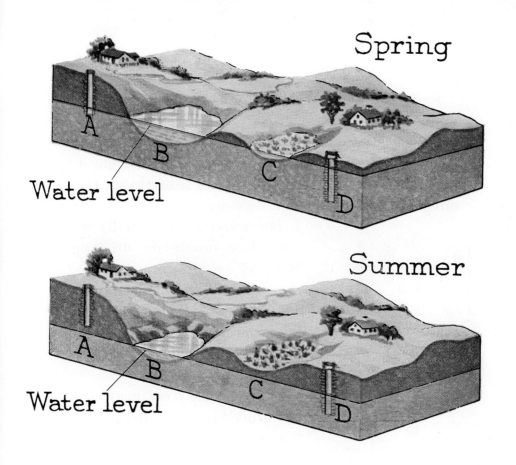

Spring

Water level

Summer

Water level

These pictures show the same piece of land during a wet season and during a dry season.

The pond at B grows smaller when there is little rain. The marsh at C dries up in dry weather but it fills up after heavy rains. Have you seen any ponds and marshes that dry up when there is little rain?

The well at D has water in it in both wet weather and in dry weather. The well at A may dry up in dry weather.

Wells

Early wells were dug out by hand. The sides were built up with stones.

Such wells were not deep and they did not go far below the water level in the soil. There might be plenty of water in these wells in wet seasons, but they often became dry in dry seasons.

The water in these wells was sometimes unsafe for drinking. Rain fell on the ground around the wells and soaked down to the water level. If there were harmful bacteria in the ground around the well, they were carried into the drinking water.

Many people were made sick by drinking water from wells that were not safe.

284

Water
level

Today, most wells are drilled by machinery. The wells are deep and often go through solid rock to layers that carry water. Find out how deep some of the new wells are around your home if you live in the country.

The wells are lined with steel pipe. Concrete is poured around the top to keep out dirty water. Such wells are usually safer than open wells.

We cannot be sure that the drinking water in any well is safe to drink unless we have it tested. The water may have come from a place where there are harmful bacteria. Health officers will test the water for you. They will tell you what to do if the water is not safe. They will tell you when to have the water tested again if it is safe to drink.

Concrete

Steel pipe

Water level

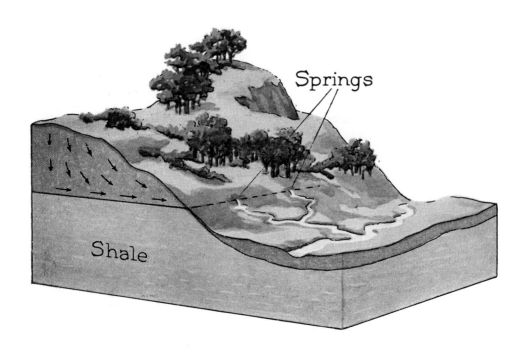

Springs

Shale

Springs

Water that falls on a hill soaks into the soil until it comes to a layer that it cannot go through. Then it flows out the side of the hill in springs.

The water from the springs usually flows down the valley in a stream. Other streams run into it and make a bigger stream.

Sometimes the water cannot run away because of the shape of the land. There may be a swamp or marsh if the water is not deep. There may be a pond or lake if the water is deep.

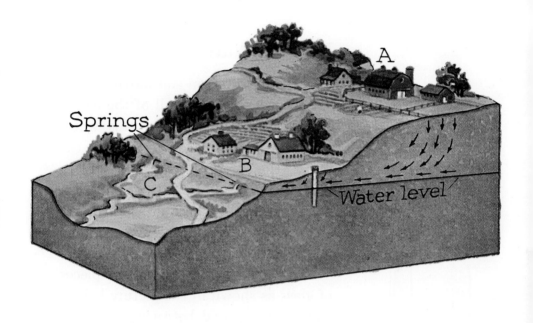

Some people think the water in springs is safe to drink because it went through the soil. This is not so. Many people have been made sick by bacteria carried in ground water.

The rain that falls on the hill in the picture comes out of the springs at C. This water may have bacteria in it from the farms at A and B. The well at B may not be safe either, because some of the water may come from the farm at A.

The only way to be sure that water in a spring or well is safe for drinking is to have it tested. If the water is not tested, boil the water before drinking it.

287

Rise of Water in Soils

Rain that falls on soil moves downward because of the pull of the earth. In dry weather, some of this water may move upward again against the pull of the earth.

Put a piece of blotting paper in colored water. There are many tiny spaces in blotting paper. Water is able to rise in these tiny spaces.

Slip a rubber band around two pieces of glass as shown in the picture below. Put a bit of wood between the pieces of glass to keep the edges apart at one side. Set the pieces of glass in a dish of colored water. Where does the water climb the highest?

288

Blotting paper

Wood

Water can rise in soil in much the same way. The water makes its way up through tiny spaces in the soil.

Test the speed with which water rises in different soils. Find two lamp chimneys. Tie a piece of paper towel on the bottom of each. Fill one chimney with dry clay. Fill the other with dry sand.

Set the chimneys in a tray. Put colored water in the tray. In which kind of soil does the water rise higher?

Minerals in Ground Water

The movement of water in soil is important to plants. During dry weather, water rises from the soaked soil far below the roots of plants. This water keeps plants alive.

Many minerals in the soil dissolve in water. Plants need some of these minerals. Water that rises through the soil brings these minerals upward.

This experiment shows how important some of the dissolved minerals in ground water are to plants. Punch small nail holes in the bottom of a tin can. Fill the can with rich garden soil. Pour rain water on the soil and catch the water that passes through.

Rain water

Soil

Put slips of house plants in this water that passed through the soil. Put other slips in rain water. Watch the slips grow. Which show the best root and leaf growth? Which are healthier after two weeks?

291

RAIN WATER

SOIL WATER

Hard Water

Rainwater

Limestone

Limestone is a common rock in some parts of the country. Much of this rock was formed from shells and other parts of sea animals that lived long ago.

Some of the minerals in limestone dissolve easily in water. Put some pieces of limestone in a cloth bag and break them into small bits with a hammer. Put the bits of limestone into a can that has small holes in the bottom. Pour rain water into the can and catch the water that drips through. Pour this same water through the limestone several times.

Filter the water through a piece of paper towel. Then put a few drops of the water on a pane of glass. Put a few drops of rain water on the glass. Let them evaporate. Is anything left on the glass?

292

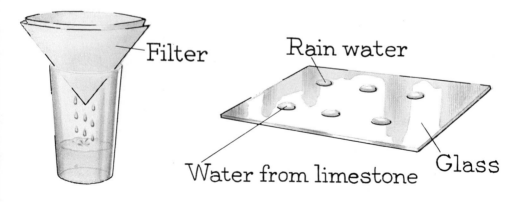

Filter

Rain water

Water from limestone

Glass

Water that has minerals from rock such as limestone dissolved in it is called "hard water." Put some hard water in one bottle and some rain water in another bottle. Add the same amount of liquid soap to each bottle. Shake the bottles well. Which bottle has the better suds? Which bottle has the clearer water?

People do not like hard water for washing. More soap is needed to make suds. The cloudy material formed in the hard water makes a ring in the bath tub and it sticks to clothing and hair.

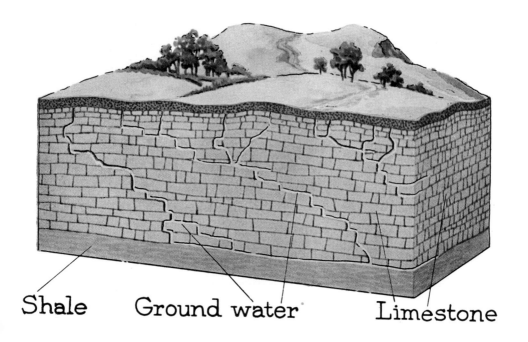

Shale   Ground water   Limestone

Limestone Caves

Water that goes into the ground usually has weak acids in it. These acids help the water dissolve limestone.

Ground water may find cracks in the beds of limestone. It trickles through the cracks. As it flows through them, it dissolves the limestone and makes the cracks larger.

In the picture above, we see that ground water is beginning to flow through cracks in the limestone. It has already made some of the cracks larger.

294

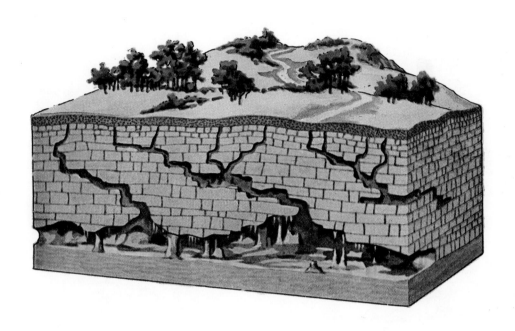

This picture shows how the same limestone may look thousands of years later. Ground water has made some of the cracks much larger. These cracks have become caves.

People can go into these caves if they find openings big enough to crawl through. Sometimes there is an opening at the top where part of the roof of a cave falls in. Sometimes people can go into the opening where the water comes out.

Suppose that the water keeps flowing through the limestone for thousands of years longer. What do you think might happen to the cave?

When people go into a cave they may find the stream
that made it. As long as the stream flows it will keep
making the cave larger.

Sometimes rocks fall across the stream. The rocks
dam up the water and make a lake. People often take
boats into the cave and travel on the underground
lake.

The streams in caves must come out somewhere.
Usually they come out as big springs. Sometimes they
come out beneath rivers and lakes.

The stream in a cave may find a new path through
cracks in the limestone. Then the old opening will be
dry. People can enter the cave through this opening
if it is large enough.

Hot Springs and Geysers

In some parts of the world there are hot rocks deep under the soil. Ground water that trickles down to these rocks becomes hot. Sometimes this water comes out in hot springs. Sometimes it is blown upward by steam as geysers

---

1. Why is it dangerous to drink water from springs that have not been tested?
2. Where does the water in a well come from?
3. What is hard water?
4. Why does the water level in the soil change through the year?
5. How can water make a cave?
6. How do plants get water in dry weather?
7. Why are dissolved minerals in ground water important to the farmer?

Fish Life

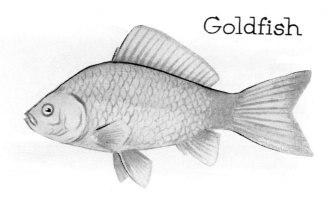

Goldfish

How a Fish Swims

A goldfish can show you many things about the way most fish swim. Study the goldfish carefully. How many fins does it have? Where are the fins?

How does the goldfish drive itself forward rapidly? How does it balance itself when it is not moving ahead? Can a goldfish swim backward? If so, which fins does it use?

Some of the fins keep the fish moving in a straight line much as feathers keep an arrow moving straight. The fins on the back and the fin below the tail help to do this.

Look at pictures of different kinds of fish. Where are the fins on these fish?

300

Fins

Bass

Does a goldfish rest on the bottom when it is quiet?
Can the fish stay in one place without moving its fins?
Does the fish begin to move up or down when it stops
moving its fins?

Perhaps you have seen a dead goldfish. Does a
dead goldfish float or sink?

Many kinds of fish have air
bladders in their bodies. An
air bladder is something like a
balloon filled with air. It helps
a fish float. The fish does not
need to swim so hard to keep
off the bottom.

A dead fish floats on its side
because the air bladder is near
the middle of the fish.

301

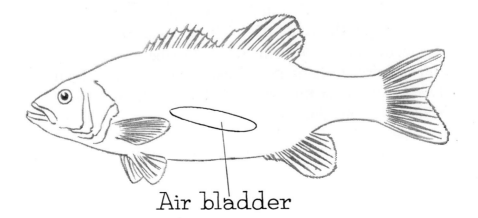

Air bladder

The Life of a Sunfish

In spring, the male sunfish begins to build a nest. He chooses a place in clear, shallow water, usually among water plants.

He waves his tail rapidly near the bottom. This washes away the mud. He picks up small stones with his mouth and carries them to the edge of the nest.

The finished nest is shaped like a saucer. It is about twice as wide as the sunfish is long. The bottom is made of clean, fine sand.

Soon a female sunfish swims into the nest. The two then swim around and around the nest. The female lays eggs. The male gives off sperms.

Then the female swims away. Sometimes other females come and lay their eggs in the nest also.

The eggs fall to the bottom. Each egg is sticky on the outside and it sticks to the sand in the nest.

The sperms fall too. They enter the eggs. Only after a sperm enters an egg can the egg develop.

303

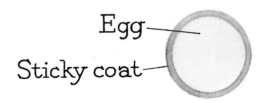

Egg

Sticky coat

A female sunfish does not take care of her young. She swims away and leaves her eggs. The male stays and takes care of the nest.

Each male guards his nest carefully. He tries to chase away other water animals that might eat the eggs. He washes away mud that falls on the eggs.

There are many dangers for the eggs. Most small water animals eat them. Salamanders, tadpoles, and almost all kinds of water insects must be kept away. Other fish, even other sunfish, will eat the eggs if the male does not guard the nest all the time.

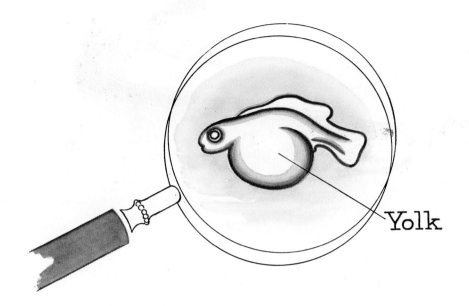

Yolk

Sunfish eggs develop rapidly. After a week of warm weather, the young sunfish begin to move about. The male stops guarding them soon afterwards.

A young sunfish does not eat at first. It uses the food in the yolk of the egg from which it grew. When the yolk is used up, it begins to feed on very tiny plants and animals.

Young sunfish have many enemies. Many meat-eating animals hunt for them. Only a few live to grow up. These are the ones that have more young in later years.

Pickerel

How Fish Get Their Food

Most fish eat animals smaller than themselves. Many kinds eat other fish, even young fish of their own kind.

Fish that catch and eat other fish usually have large mouths. Some of them can swallow fish half as long as themselves.

Such fish usually have sharp teeth. They use the teeth to hold the animals they catch. They do not chew with these teeth. They swallow their food whole.

306

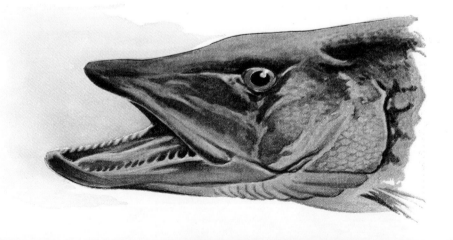

Perch

Many fish eat insects that are on water plants. They get these insects by sucking them in with a mouthful of water. These fish also eat insects that fall on top of the water. Such fish usually have their mouths on the front of their heads. How is this helpful to them?

Fish called suckers eat tiny plants and animals that live on the bottoms of ponds and streams. A sucker puts its mouth against the bottom and sucks in its food. Notice the shape of the sucker's mouth. Notice where the mouth is. How is this helpful to the sucker?

307

Killifish

Sucker

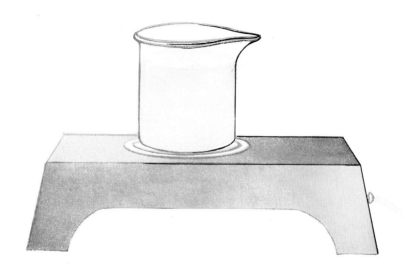

Oxygen and Fish

Oxygen is a gas that is important to all animals. They must have it so that they can use the energy in their foods.

Land animals get their oxygen from the air. Fish and many other water animals use oxygen that is dissolved in water.

Heating water drives out oxygen and other gases dissolved in it. Put some cold water in a glass cooking dish and heat it. In a few minutes you will see bubbles on the sides of the dish. These are bubbles of oxygen and other gases that are leaving the water.

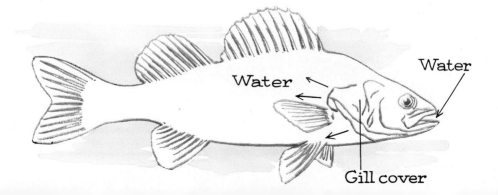

Water

Water

Gill cover

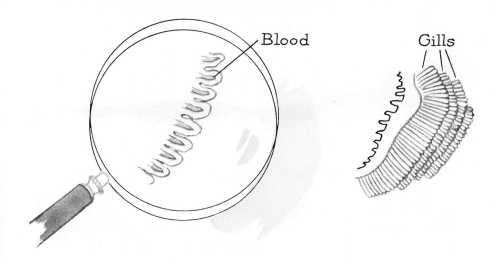

Blood

Gills

Fish take the oxygen from the water with their gills. The gills are in the back part of a fish's head under the gill covers.

The fish takes in fresh water through its mouth. This water passes around the gills and goes out slits behind the gill covers.

The skin on the gills is very thin and there is blood close to the surface. Oxygen is able to go from the water through this thin skin. The blood carries the oxygen to all parts of the fish's body.

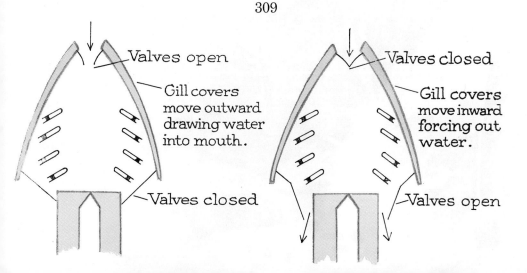

Valves open

Gill covers move outward drawing water into mouth.

Valves closed

Valves closed

Gill covers move inward forcing out water.

Valves open

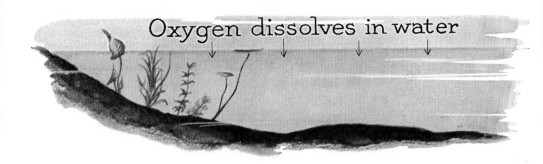
Oxygen dissolves in water

How Oxygen Gets into the Water

Probably most of the oxygen in water comes from the oxygen in the air. This oxygen dissolves into the water at the top of a pond or a slow stream. Tests show that there is more oxygen in the upper part of a pond than at the bottom.

In swift streams, bubbles of air are carried under water. Some of the oxygen in the bubbles dissolves into the water. Swift streams usually have more oxygen than quiet streams and ponds.

How do waterfalls help add oxygen to the water?

310

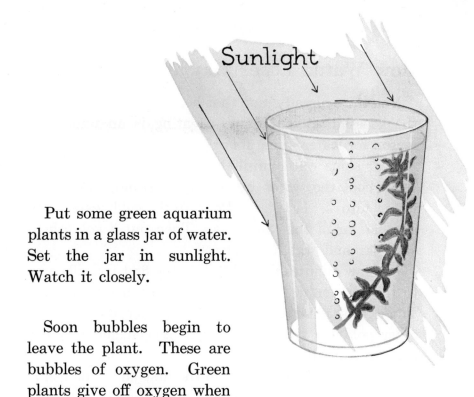

Sunlight

Put some green aquarium plants in a glass jar of water. Set the jar in sunlight. Watch it closely.

Soon bubbles begin to leave the plant. These are bubbles of oxygen. Green plants give off oxygen when they are making sugar in sunlight.

The oxygen given off by green plants dissolves in the water. If there are many green plants in ponds or streams, part of the oxygen in the water comes from the plants while they are making food.

311

Oxygen from plants in sunlight

How Water Loses Oxygen

You have already seen that heating water drives out the gases dissolved in it. Heating is an important reason for water losing its oxygen.

Heat some water until the gases have bubbled out. Then cool the water by letting it stand. Pour the water into a glass jar. Pour fresh, cold water into another jar of the same size. Then put a goldfish in each jar and watch closely.

In a few minutes the goldfish in the first jar will come to the top for water that has oxygen dissolved in it. There was not enough oxygen farther down. The other goldfish will have enough oxygen and will not need to come to the top.

Do not leave the goldfish in the first jar. The fish is uncomfortable there and it may even die.

312

Water that has been heated and then cooled   Cool, fresh water

Live
animals

Animals that live in ponds and streams use some of the oxygen dissolved in the water. If there are many animals, they may use up most of it. Sometimes we put too many animals in one aquarium and then the animals die because there is not enough oxygen.

Some kinds of bacteria use oxygen from the water. The bacteria that causes dead things to decay are important because there may be so many of them. There may be countless millions of these bacteria in streams where sewage and garbage are dumped.

Dead plants
and animals

Conservation of Fishing

Above is a picture of a stream that you might find in many places. All the trees and bushes have been cut down. Below is a picture of the same stream as it might look if trees and bushes were growing along its banks.

Which stream becomes warmer in summer? Which stream digs away its banks and becomes muddy? Which stream is better for fish? Give the reasons for your answers.

Sometimes people buy the land around the headwaters of good fishing streams. They plant trees and let the bushes grow. Tell how this helps. How are people other than fishermen helped by this?

Here are two ways that fishing can be spoiled. A city may dump its garbage into the river. It may also run its sewer into the river. Why is this bad for animals that live in the river? What are some other reasons people should not do this?

Most states have conservation departments that try to protect the streams. They try to keep cities from dumping garbage and sewage in the streams. They try to keep factories from dumping chemicals into the streams. They try to keep sawmills from dumping sawdust in the streams.

Does your state have a conservation department? Find out what it does to protect the streams in your state.

Oxygen in Aquariums

Here are two kinds of aquariums. In which one does more of the water touch the air? In which one will oxygen dissolve faster?

There may be several places where you can keep an aquarium. One place might be above a radiator. Another place might be in a sunny window. Another might be in a window that faces north. Which place do you think is best for an aquarium?

316

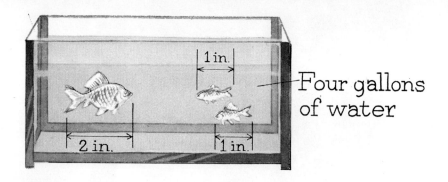

Four gallons
of water

1 in.

2 in.

1 in.

Each fish should have enough water so it will be sure of having oxygen. A good rule is to use a gallon of water for each fish an inch long, two gallons of water for each fish two inches long, and so on.

Always take out dead plants and animals and uneaten food as soon as possible. Why?

Here is a way to take uneaten food from an aquarium. Hold a glass tube as shown and lower it to the bottom. Take your finger from the top. Water and uneaten food will enter the tube. Then put your finger back on the tube and lift it from the water.

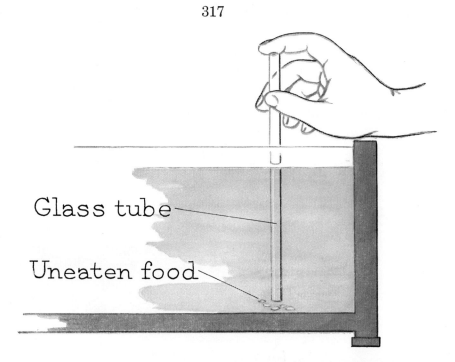

Glass tube

Uneaten food

Brook Trout

Brook trout are fish that need much oxygen. They can live only in cold lakes and swift, cool streams.

Why is it that brook trout cannot live in warm ponds and streams? Why do they die when sewage and garbage are dumped into the streams where they live?

Brook trout lay their eggs in late fall. They swim up cold streams as far as they can. They make nests somewhat as sunfish do. The females lay their eggs. The males give off sperms. Then the trout cover the eggs with gravel. The males may guard the nests for a few days before they leave them.

Trout

Fishermen like to catch trout, but so many streams have been spoiled for fishing that there are not enough trout for all the fishermen.

Conservation departments in some states have built fish hatcheries to raise young trout.

Full grown trout are kept in pools of cold running water. During the egg-laying season, men squeeze eggs from the females and sperms from the males. The eggs and sperms are mixed in pails.

Then the eggs are put in trays of cold running water. After the eggs hatch, the young fish are fed carefully until they are three or four inches long. Then they are put in cold streams and lakes.

319

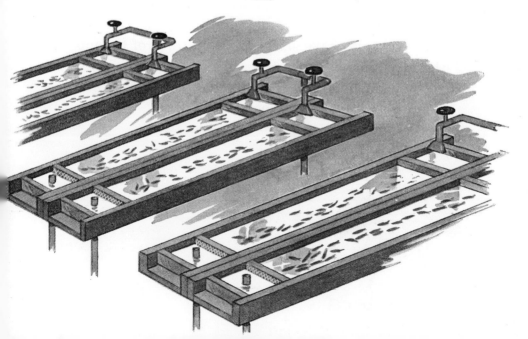

Sharp spines

Bullhead

Bullheads

Bullheads need less oxygen than many other kinds of fish. They can live on the bottoms of warm, muddy ponds.

Different kinds of bullheads have many names. Sometimes they are called "horned pout," "mud cats," and "catfish."

Bullheads usually lie on the bottom of a pond. Their eyes are small. Perhaps they do not need large eyes in muddy water. They have four pairs of "feelers" that look like cats' whiskers. The feelers seem to be used in finding food in the mud.

Bullheads also have sharp spines in three of the fins. Fishermen should know how to pick up bullheads so that they do not hurt their hands.

320

Feelers

The male and the female bullhead build the nest together. They move pebbles and bits of sticks from the nest. They wash away some of the mud. The finished nest looks a little like the nest of the sunfish.

The female lays her eggs and the male gives off sperms. Then the male guards the nest. When the eggs hatch, the male guards the young bullheads for several days.

Most kinds of bullheads are small, but there are kinds that grow large. The catfish in the Mississippi sometimes weigh more than 100 pounds.

321

Salmon

Fish That Migrate

A number of fish migrate into shallow streams to lay their eggs just as brook trout do. One of the most important of these is the salmon of the Pacific Coast. These salmon live in the ocean most of their lives. In the fall, when they are full grown, the salmon swim up the rivers. They may go up for hundreds of miles.

They lay their eggs and give off sperms in shallow water near the upper ends of the streams. Then they die.

The young fish live in the streams until they are a few inches long. Then they swim to the ocean. When they are full grown they swim back up the same streams they came down.

Salmon are caught in great numbers as they go up the streams. At one time there was danger that the salmon would be wiped out, but laws now protect them. Now a great danger is from dams that keep the fish from going up the streams to lay their eggs.

322

A different kind of salmon lives on the Atlantic Coast. These fish do not die when they lay their eggs. They swim back to the ocean again.

However, most of the rivers in the United States are no longer fit for the Atlantic salmon because of sewage, chemicals from factories, and dams across the rivers. There are still some good rivers for them in Canada.

The shad is another fish that migrates up the rivers of the Atlantic Coast. Shad spend most of their lives in the Atlantic Ocean. They go up the rivers in spring to lay their eggs. There were once many more shad than there are now. Many rivers have become too dirty for shad.

323

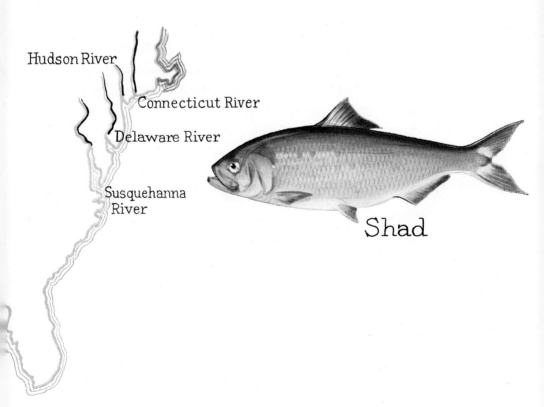

Hudson River

Connecticut River

Delaware River

Susquehanna River

Shad

Eel

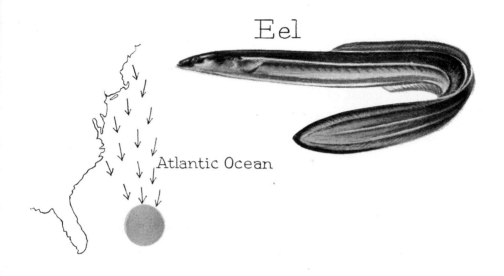

Atlantic Ocean

Eels look a little like snakes but they are really fish. Eels have fins and gills like other fish.

Eels migrate, but much differently from the fish you have been studying. Eels live near the headwaters of streams most of their lives. When they are full grown they migrate to the ocean to lay their eggs. The young eels then swim back up the streams.

---

1. What do most fresh water fish eat?
2. What must happen to a fish egg before it can develop?
3. How does oxygen get into water?
4. How does a fish get the oxygen it needs?
5. Why does garbage and sewage spoil fishing?
6. Where is the best place in a house to keep an aquarium?

Trees

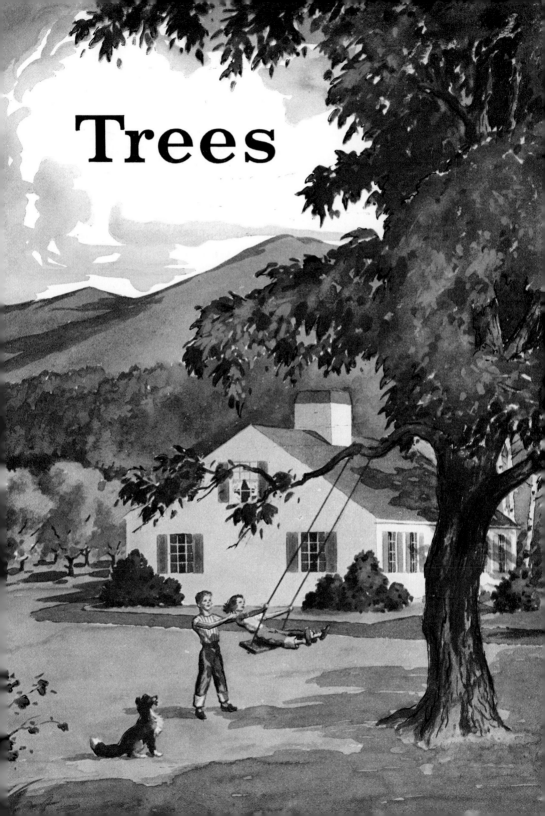

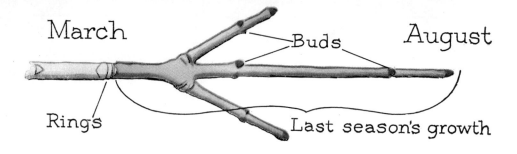

March

Buds

August

Rings

Last season's growth

How a Tree Grows

Look at a twig from any small tree. Notice that the end of the twig is a lighter color than the rest of the twig. It is often light green. This is the part of the twig that grew during the last growing season. There are often rings that show where each season's growth ended.

One twig may grow only a few inches during a season. But if you could add together the growth of all the twigs on one tree, you would find that the tree grew many feet each season.

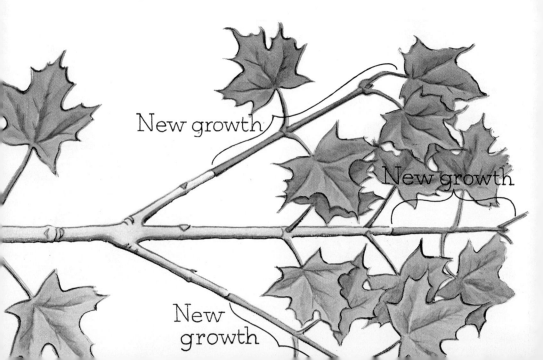

New growth

New growth

New growth

The trunk and twigs of a tree not only grow longer but they also grow bigger around. Each year, a tree adds a layer of wood beneath its bark.

Peel the bark from a live twig. Notice the green layer beneath the bark. This is where the tree is growing bigger around. Wood is made in this layer during the spring and summer.

If you cut through a tree trunk or large limb, you will see rings in the wood. These rings are the layers of wood that are added each year. The light-colored layer was made in the spring when the tree grew rapidly. The hard, dark ring was made when the tree grew more slowly during the summer.

You can find out how old a tree is by counting the rings in the trunk. How old is the tree shown below?

Spring growth

Summer growth

One year's growth

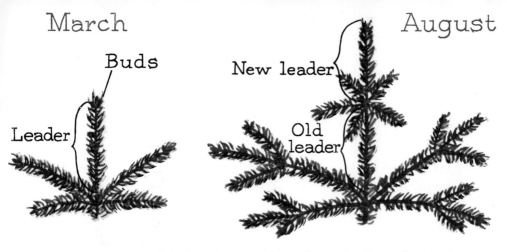

March · Buds · Leader · New leader · August · Old leader

In many kinds of trees there is a single twig in the center that grows upward. This twig is called the leader. The other twigs grow outward.

The leader grows upward during the spring and summer. During the summer new buds form on its upper end. The top bud becomes the leader during the next growing season. The other buds become side branches.

You can often tell the age of young pine trees or spruce trees by counting the spaces between branches on the trunk of each tree. Each space represents one of the leaders in past years.

New growth

Growth last year

Growth two years ago

Growth three years ago

Growth four years ago

Growth five years ago

The leader of one of these trees may be killed by freezing, by insects that lay their eggs in the buds, or by animals that eat the buds. Then a side twig usually turns upward and becomes a new leader. For a few years there will be a bend in the trunk where the side branch turned upward. In time, however, the trunk grows large and the bend disappears.

New leader

Dead leader bud

Sometimes two or more side branches turn upward. Then there is more than one leader. Look for evergreen trees that have more than one leader. Why are such trees worth little for lumber?

329

The Shapes of Trees

The shape of a tree depends upon how many of its twigs grow upward. Some kinds send up one main twig. A tree of this type has a trunk that rises through the center of the tree almost to the top.

Other kinds of trees send several twigs upward. A tree of this type has a short trunk that divides into many branches.

Look at trees growing near your school. Find trees of each type. Try to learn their names.

330

Oak   Elm

Maple tree in a field   Maple trees in a thick woods

The shape of a tree also depends upon whether it is growing in the open or in a thick woods. Above are pictures of maple trees. The tree growing in the open has light coming from all sides. Each twig grows longer and larger. Notice the shape of the tree.

The trees growing in the woods have plenty of light only at the top. The lower twigs die. The upper branches grow upward. Notice the shape of these trees. Which trees will make better lumber?

Look at twigs that are shaded by other twigs. Are some of them dead? Are some of them dying?

331

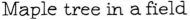

A low branch of a
maple tree

Oak leaf   Ash leaf

The Leaves of Trees

The leaves of trees have many shapes. Some are almost round. Some have edges like saw teeth. Some are divided into several smaller parts. Some are shaped like needles. You can tell one kind of tree from another by the leaves.

Tree leaves make the food that the trees need. They make it from water and air. They use energy from sunlight.

Many kinds of trees lose their leaves at the end of the growing season. A corky layer grows at the end of each leaf stalk. Water stops rising into the leaf and the leaf dies. The color often changes to red, orange, yellow, or brown. Then the leaf falls off.

332

Maple

Corky layer

Spruce

Hemlock

Cedar

Other kinds of trees keep their leaves through the winter. These trees are called evergreens. Look for evergreen trees and learn their names.

Evergreens, such as pines and spruces, have leaves like needles. Others, such as cedars, have leaves shaped like scales. The seeds of these trees grow in cones.

Most of the cone-bearing trees keep their leaves several years. The pine twig shown below has needles that grew in three different seasons. The new needles are on the newest growth between B and A. Last season's needles are still on the twig that grew between C and B. The needles that grew two seasons ago are falling from the twig between D and C. All the needles have fallen from the twig that grew three seasons ago.

333

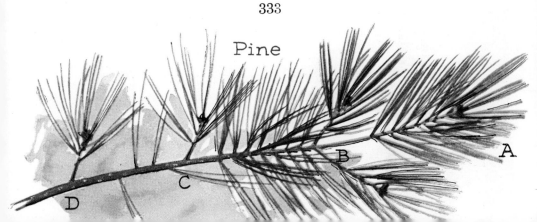

Pine

Black knot
on twigs
of plum tree

Enemies of Trees

Among the many enemies of trees are small plants that live inside the trees. These plants are called **parasites.** They use the tree for food. Usually they harm the trees, and sometimes they kill the trees.

Perhaps you have seen black growths on plum trees. These are parts of small plants living inside the twigs. The black parts give off spores that are carried by the wind to other plum trees.

When you see shelf mushrooms growing on living trees you know that there are parasites living in the trees. The shelves are parts of the parasites. They give off spores that are blown to other trees.

334

Shelf mushrooms

Dead
chestnut
trees

Fifty years ago the trees in this picture were healthy chestnut trees. Chestnuts were one of this country's favorite nuts. Chestnut lumber was used for many things.

Nearly all of these chestnut trees have been killed by tiny parasites. The parasites were brought in from Asia where they grew on another kind of chestnut tree. They killed the growing layer under the bark of our chestnut trees.

There are many other kinds of parasites that kill trees. Some of these parasites are carried by the wind from one tree to another. Other parasites are carried by insects. Elm trees are being killed by parasites carried by beetles that burrow under the bark of the trees.

335

Work of grubs of Dutch elm beetles

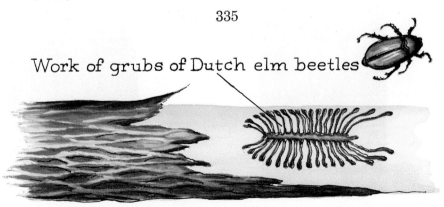

After a
wind storm

Tree Injuries

Trees are easily injured. Strong winds may tear off some of the branches. People may knock off some of the bark or cut the bark with knives and axes. How else may trees be injured?

A tree can heal a small injury in a few years. The growing layer under the bark spreads out over the injury. It makes new wood and new bark. In a few years only a scar remains.

Look for scars on trees to see how the tree heals small injuries.

336

Two years later

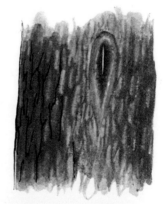

Five years later

Rotting wood

Large injuries need several years before they are healed. During these years, spores from parasites may fall on the wood and begin to grow. These parasites make the wood decay.

Nearly all the wood in the center of a tree may rot away and leave the tree hollow. Such a tree has no value for lumber. The tree is weak and can easily be damaged by strong winds.

Many animals are helped by hollow trees. Raccoons use hollow trees for dens. Some insects spend the winter in hollow trees. Name other animals that use hollow trees.

337

Hollow in rotting wood

Lumber

Lumber is one of our most important building materials. List some ways that lumber is used.

The best lumber comes from straight, tall trees. Hollow trees, crooked trees, and small trees do not make good lumber.

The good trees are cut down and sawed into logs. The logs are then taken to the sawmills.

Much of the tree cannot be used for lumber. Part of the tree may be cut into firewood. The rest of the tree is wasted. More than a half of every tree is wasted.

338

Stump   Saw logs   Firewood   Waste

At the sawmill a log is put on a car that runs on tracks. The car pushes the log against the saw.

The boards cut from the outside of a log have bark on them. Such boards are usually used for firewood. After the outside boards are sawed off, a few more boards are cut from each side of the log. The picture below shows the order in which they are usually cut.

The center boards are usually worth less than the outer boards. The center of the log was the trunk of the tree when it was young and when there were many side branches. Therefore, the center boards have more knots in them than the outer boards do.

Grain in Lumber

Look at boards in tables and other woodwork. Notice the pattern of light and dark wood. This pattern is called the grain of the wood. Can you find any boards that have no grain?

The grain is caused by sawing through the growth rings of a log. Imagine that you can see a log after one board has been sawed from it as in the picture below. Notice the growth rings in the end of the log and follow some of them along the side where the board was taken off.

Look at the growth rings in the end of a board. Follow some of them along the side of the board.

340

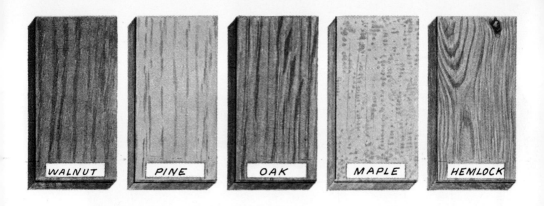

WALNUT   PINE   OAK   MAPLE   HEMLOCK

Different kinds of wood have different kinds of grain. Visit a lumber yard or a woodworking shop and study the different kinds of wood. Notice how the grain in each kind looks.

Collect small pieces of different kinds of wood. Smooth one side of each piece with sandpaper to make the grain show better. Label your collection.

You may find dark spots called knots in some of your boards. Notice the grain around a knot. A knot marks the place where there was a branch on a tree. The picture helps you understand why a knot shows when a board is sawed from the tree trunk.

Knot

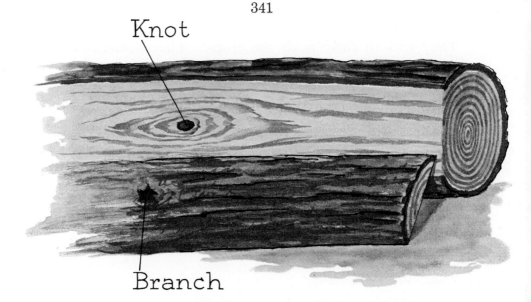

Branch

Forests in the United States

When people from Europe first came to this country, they found great forests of large, straight trees. They often had to cut trees to make places for their houses. They had to clear fields for crops. They sometimes piled up the trees and burned them just to get rid of them.

Until about 1850, however, there were still great forests in the East except in good farming land. The forests of the West had not been touched until that time. It seemed as though there would always be plenty of lumber.

Today the picture is different. The great eastern forests were almost completely cut down before 1900. The forests that remain are made up mostly of small trees that do not make good lumber.

There are still some large forests in the West, and most of the good lumber trees are in these forests. But all our forests are being cut rapidly.

Some of the western forests are owned by the national government. However, over half the land in the national forests is in such rough or dry country that it will never raise good lumber trees. We cannot depend upon our national forests for the lumber we will need in the future. We must show the people who own their own land how to make better use of their forests.

343

Destruction and Conservation of Forests

We are using our trees much faster than new ones can grow. A tree must grow for over a hundred years to make a high grade of lumber. It must grow about fifty years to make paper pulp.

One of the reasons our forests continue to disappear is that we waste too much. We allow too many forest fires. We allow too many homes to burn. We bring in parasites that kill our trees. We cut trees that are too small and we waste a large part of the wood in each tree.

Our national and state governments are trying to show how trees can be used more wisely. They try to prevent forest fires. They study tree parasites to find out how to control them. They experiment with better ways to cut and use trees.

Our governments are also setting aside forests that should not be cut because the trees help hold soil and water on the mountains. Find out what your state government is doing to conserve its forests.

Loose soil

How to Plant a Tree

Dig a hole that is a foot deeper and a foot wider than the roots of the tree. Loosen the soil in the bottom of the hole and put in some well rotted leaves or manure.

Set the tree in the hole. The roots should be at the same level as they were before the tree was dug up. Put some soil around the roots to hold them and fill the hole with water. Then put in the rest of the soil and pack it tightly with your feet. Keep the tree well watered.

---

1. How does a tree grow larger?
2. What makes the grain in wood?
3. Why are leaves important to trees?
4. Why are trees important to us?
5. Why are our good forests disappearing?
6. How can you help prevent forest fires?
7. What is being done to conserve our forests?

The Major Topics Presented in Each Unit

*Unit 1 — Plants That Are Not Green. How non-green plants get their food. How non-green plants reproduce. How non-green plants do both good and harm.

Unit 2 — Saving the Soil. Why topsoil is important. How topsoil is being lost. How topsoil can be protected and restored.

*Unit 3 — Time and Seasons. How time is determined. What causes change of seasons. How seasonal changes affect living things.

*Unit 4 — Our Eyes. How our eyes are protected from injuries. How to take care of our eyes. How we see. How the eyes of animals compare with ours.

Unit 5 — Making Work Easier. Some common ways of doing work more easily. How some common tools work. How friction can be reduced.

Unit 6 — Musical Sounds. How musical sounds are produced. Some common musical instruments. How people make and hear sounds.

*Unit 7 — Some Common Acids. Acids in our daily lives. How to test for acids. How acids affect the things about us.

Unit 8 — Electromagnets. What electromagnets are. How electromagnetism can be changed. How electromagnets are used.

Unit 9 — Bird Study. What birds are like. How birds differ. How birds take care of their young.

Unit 10 — How Airplanes Fly. How airplanes are controlled. The forces that act on an airplane. How airplanes are given energy to fly.

*Unit 11 — Warm Air in Motion. What happens when air is heated. Causes of the unequal heating of air. Effects of air currents.

*Unit 12 — Water in the Ground. What happens to the water that goes into the soil. What wells and springs are. What ground water does to the rocks it flows through.

Unit 13 — Fish Life. How fish are adapted for a life in water. How fish reproduce. What factors harm fish.

Unit 14 — Trees. How trees grow. How trees are injured. How lumber is produced. How we can protect our forests.

* These units include health and safety material.

Index

348

curdle, 168–169
curds, 169
cylinder, 238

dams, 49
deadly amanita, 12
decay, 30, 178, 313
deermouse, 102
delta wing, 248
derrick, 105
destroying angel, 12
digestion, 170–171
dog, 92
dough, 24–25
dragonfly, 104
dry cell, 182–191, 194, 196
duck, 221, 223
dust, 52

ears, 157
earth, 56–59, 62–63, 66–67, 76–79
earthworm, 30
east, 57, 66–67
eel, 324
eggs, 220–221, 303–305, 318–319, 321, 324
elm, 330, 335
energy, 10, 130, 199, 200, 332
electrical bells, 196–197
    buzzers, 196–197
    charges, 275
electricity, 181–200
electric lights, 74
    motor, 198–199
electromagnets, 181–200
elevators, 230–231
engine, 238–239
English sparrow, 202, 209
erosion, 27–52, 176–177, 294–297
evaporate, 271, 278–279, 282
evergreen tree, 328–329, 333
eye, 81–104, 320

fairy ring mushrooms, 13
farsightedness, 97

feathers, 214–217
female, 208–209, 220–223, 224, 303–304, 318–319, 321
fern, 178
fins, 300, 320, 324
fire, 38, 40–41, 160, 174–175, 254–255
fire extinguisher, 174–175
fish, 101, 279, 299–324
    hatchery, 319
flight, 216–217
flour, 165–167, 170
flute, 150
fly amanita, 12
forest, 342–345
    fire, 40–41, 344–345
French horn, 153
friction, 126–129
frog, 100
fruit, 19
fuel, 239
fungi, 4–26

gases, 161, 308–320
gasoline, 130, 238
generator, 200
geyser, 298
gills, 309, 324
glasses, 97
globe, 56, 63, 76–79
goldenrod, 74
goldfinch, 75, 208
goldfish, 100, 300–301, 312–313
goldthread, 178
grain, 340–341
grapefruit, 162
grass, 32, 38–39, 42–44, 46
grease, 127–128
greenhouse, 74
grouse, 223
guitar, 138, 140
gullies, 29, 34–35, 42–46, 48–49
gulls, 203, 217

hail, 274
hammer, 121
hard water, 292–293

350

351

ROI